Raising
Topsy-Turvy Kids

Successfully Parenting
Your
Visual-Spatial Child

Raising Topsy-Turvy Kids

Successfully Parenting Your Visual-Spatial Child

Alexandra Shires Golon

With a foreword by
Linda Kreger Silverman, Ph.D.

DeLeon Publishing
DENVER, COLORADO

Published by:
DeLeon Publishing, Inc.
P.O. Box 461027
Denver, CO 80246
www.deleonpub.com

ISBN 1-932186-08-5   (pbk)
04 05 06 07 08   0 9 8 7 6 5 4 3 2 1

Dedication

To Sam and Matt, the most important topsy-turvy kids
in my life. To their father, my incredible husband,
a topsy-turvy kid at heart. And, especially, to Linda,
without whom I would have had no idea the gifts
my children possess, nor how best to honor
and nurture them.

TABLE OF CONTENTS

Chapter One

Chapter Two

Chapter Three

Chapter Four

Chapter Five

Chapter Six

Chapter Seven

References

Appendix A

Appendix B

Appendix C

Index

Figures & Charts

Acknowledgments

I was simultaneously thrilled and apprehensive when I was asked to write a companion book on parenting visual-spatial learners. Despite living with two topsy-turvy children and an extremely visual-spatial husband, it can be daunting to write a book on your family life, particularly while viewing it through the lens of someone else's theory on learning styles. It is with the deepest gratitude that I mention my very special friend and someone I love as an adopted mom, Linda Silverman, author of **Upside-Down Brilliance: The Visual-Spatial Learner** and creator of the visual-spatial learner concept. It has been an honor and a privilege to serve as her "right hand" for the last several years. Her insights have helped me to better understand and successfully raise my own children.

Thank you to Bill, Sam and Matt (my guys), three of the most visual-spatial people I have ever met or had the pleasure to live with! I hope they'll forgive me for sharing so much of their lives within these pages.

Thanks to Buck Jones for illustrations that matched or went beyond my wildest imagination. Buck is truly a visual-spatial adult who has found his calling.

Many thanks, also, to the parents of topsy-turvy children who wrote to me offering their tips and suggestions for successful parenting. It is so inspiring to hear your tales of love and support. And a special thank you to the children themselves for persevering in what, until now, must have seemed an inhospitable environment. It is with great hope that your special strengths will continue to be recognized and honored as we still have much to learn from you.

Foreword

When I started writing **Upside-Down Brilliance: The Visual-Spatial Learner**, my plan was to write a short book for parents with no references. It just didn't turn out that way. As a recovering academic, I found it impossible to write anything without citations! And since it was the first book I had written on a concept I had developed over a 20-year period, I felt compelled to include all the theoretical under-pinnings; methods of clinical assessment; research on the *Visual-Spatial Identifier*; the introverted personality type often found in visual-spatial learners (VSLs); the interaction of VSLs with giftedness, learning disabilities and AD/HD; tons of teaching techniques; and, to my surprise, a chapter on VSL adults. The book clearly had its own agenda—I was just the scribe.

Raising Topsy-Turvy Kids is the book I wanted to write. But I'm glad that Allie Golon wrote it. She actually knows the visual-spatial construct better than I do! In addition to reading and re-reading copious drafts of **Upside-Down Brilliance**, Allie is an artist living with an entire family of VSLs. She has infused the book with marvelous stories about her sons, Sam and Matt, and her husband, Bill, as well as delicious anecdotes she has obtained from parents through the many listserves in which she participates. **Raising Topsy-Turvy Kids** is a joy to read.

We've used some of the same cartoons in **Upside-Down Brilliance** and **Raising Topsy-Turvy Kids** because Allie came up with most of the ideas for Buck Jones' illustrations. Despite the surface similarities, the books are really quite different from each other. Allie brings a fresh perspective and offers countless ideas to parents of VSLs. Every chapter is filled with suggestions that parents can implement immediately. The book is a treasure-trove!

   Parents can discover if their child is visual-spatial very quickly by glancing at the quiz on page 17: "*Is Your Child a Visual-Spatial Learner?*" in Chapter 2. The rest of the chapter is devoted to further exploration of the checklist, complete with anecdotes and helpful parenting tips. Chapter 3 covers the most difficult aspects of dealing with visual-spatial children on the home front: chores, getting them off to school in the morning; bedtime; visual-spatials and auditory-sequentials in the same family. Chapters 5 and 6 concentrate on parent advocacy in the schools, including practical hints for helping them stay focused, reading methods, spelling secrets, writing clues, keyboarding, organizational skills, math facts without memorization, and the bane of their existence: homework

   At this point in time, schools tend to be focused on the left-hemispheric skills of reading (phonetically), writing (by hand), and arithmetic (calculation and rote memorization). VSLs often are crushed in traditional classrooms, where they are evaluated on the basis of their left-hemispheric abilities, while their right-hemispheric brilliance is ignored. When parents find themselves against a brick wall, after they have tried valiantly to get school personnel to understand their child's learning style, it is time to consider alternatives. Allie homeschooled her boys for five years, and she has a wealth of experience to share with readers on this subject. She addresses the pros and cons of homeschooling, unschooling, partial homeschooling and afterschooling. Homeschoolers will love her list of resources in Appendix B.

   Allie and I are hopeful that in the near future schools will become more responsive to VSLs. Most educators that I have addressed in the last few years are familiar with the term, "visual-spatial learner." Some are identifying these children on their own and trying to accommodate them with more visually presented information; encouragement to create visual images in their minds in response to instruction; fewer timed tests; reduced drill and repetition; less emphasis on making students show their work; grading ideas separately from the mechanics of spelling, grammar and punctuation; substitution of more creative work than a written paper to demonstrate mastery; and more reliance on the computer. Teachers want to reach these children; they just need more support. We encourage parents to share our books with educators and to acknowledge all the teachers who are accommodating to their children's learning style.

I know you will enjoy **Raising Topsy-Turvy Kids**. Happy reading!

Linda Kreger Silverman, Ph.D.

Author, **Upside-Down Brilliance: The Visual-Spatial Learner**

Introduction

I am the proud parent of two great kids: Sam and Matt. At the time of this writing they are eleven and nine, respectively. I wrote this book for parents of children like mine. Children who would rather spend the day with a new box of LEGOs™ than do nearly anything else in the world. Kids who can get so absolutely absorbed in creative play and art of any medium that they lose all sense of time. Kids who can find joy and appreciation in watching the bugs in the grass and don't need to seek outside stimulation from video games or TV—excitement is all around them. Children who are obviously bright and can tell you the inner workings of your computer, refrigerator or vacuum. The same children, however, who don't do well on standardized tests and are not always recognized in the classroom for the gifts they possess.

Perhaps you found this book because you have a hunch that your child is a visual-spatial learner. Perhaps someone recommended it to you based on something your child said or did. Maybe you've heard the term, "visual-spatial," and now you're wondering whether this learning style explains why your kid doesn't seem to learn the same way others do. Whether your concern is for your own child or you are the care provider of a visual-spatial child, you already know that there are key differences in how this little being responds to his or her environment. In this book, "your child" refers to any child whose care is entrusted to you. Regardless of your relationship, be it as a parent, grandparent, care provider, teacher or mentor, you care enough to have pursued learning more about how they acquire and process information and so, this book is for you. On behalf of visual-spatial learners everywhere, thank you. The increased awareness of their special gifts can only bring positive changes to the classroom, to their home and to the world in which they will learn, grow and succeed. I'll detail specific characteristics of this learning style, as well as tips for identifying whether your children are visual-spatial, in Chapter 2 but, first let's discuss why it's important for you and your children to understand what it means to be a visual-spatial learner.

Often labeled disorganized, unfocused, poor spellers or worse, these "topsy-turvy" kids can be equal parts pleasure and frustration to raise. What I call "topsy-turvy" others have termed "upside-down," "right-brained" and "Edison-like." There is not much material available to address the needs of these children and what does exist is aimed primarily at teachers and the challenges these kids bring to the classroom. But I know firsthand how demanding it can be to maintain harmony at home, too.

In my travels with Linda Silverman, author of **Upside-Down Brilliance: The Visual-Spatial Learner**, I have spoken with a great many parents of this type of learner. Most just want to know some bit of advice for raising their topsy-turvy kids; they want to know they are not alone in parenting these unpredictable, often brilliant, children. They want to know how to advocate effectively for their children's needs and to know that even if their children are not successful in school, they still hold promising futures.

In this book, I want to share what's worked and what hasn't, what's helped at various stages of development and what has failed. Success stories from my family and our home, and from other families as well. **Raising Topsy-Turvy Kids** was written specifically for parents, as a companion to **Upside-Down Brilliance**. Hopefully, it will serve as a guide, a support and a resource for successfully parenting your visual-spatial child. You'll find stories about identifying, nurturing and teaching these remarkable children throughout. Children who share a state of being utterly unpredictable, totally out-of-sync with their age peers, blissfully unaware of time ...*topsy-turvy*!

Have You Got Topsy-Turvy Children?

Topsy-turvy kids, or visual-spatial learners, are the delightful little darlings (and big darlings, too, as it seems you can't outgrow this) in our lives who crave time with such joys as building, painting, drawing, daydreaming, dancing, music making and letting their creative imaginations soar. They have little inclination to put their clothes away, or to maintain some degree of organization and you can forget about punctuality altogether. They have the most incredible moments of discovery, invention and problem solving but the skills of managing a time schedule or showing their work may absolutely elude them. They march to their own drummer and virtually nothing you do will convince them that they should change. I'm not sure they could change if they wanted to. It's all in the wiring; it's who they are. And even if we could change them, I'm certain we wouldn't really want to. If there were no visual-spatial learners among us we'd be without art and dance, without science and invention, without drama and choreography, without most of the things that make life beautiful.

Why is it important to know if your children are visual-spatial learners?

Does it matter whether or not you know your children are visual-spatial learners? Well, one might just as easily ask, does it matter whether or not you know if they are right- or left-handed? When we know children are left-handed, we don't insist that they use right-handed scissors. We used to, but now we know that lefties are born that way, that there's nothing wrong with being a leftie and we, the right-handers of the world, finally accepted lefties as they are. When given the proper tools, the tasks become easier, the job more interesting and the end results more pleasing. We now honor preferred handedness in everyone.

What if we're not giving the appropriate tools to children to match their specific learning styles? Are we dishonoring our children's hemispheres? If you, your children's teachers and others involved in their lives, understand that children can and do have preferred learning styles, and that these children could be easily taught and communicated with in their preferred learning style, wouldn't we be offering visual-spatial children the same accommodation for learning that appropriate scissors provide to preferred handedness? And if you didn't offer that tool—communicating the way that child learned and thought—could you rightfully expect a successful outcome? With the majority of teachers, curriculum and classrooms operating in an auditory-sequential style (in a step-by-step fashion, where to not show one's work is to lose at least half the credit), how can we expect visual-spatial children to thrive?

Identifying my own kids

I didn't know people actually thought and learned differently until Matt, my youngest son, was old enough to describe for me exactly how his mind works. One night, as I was tucking him in, I asked him which goodnight song he wanted. He sat straight up in bed and stared intently at the ceiling. "What are you looking at?" I asked. "My song list!" he replied. "Oh, what does it look like?" He proceeded to "draw" with his finger in the air a sort of L-shaped shelf holding every picture of every song he knew. He described the images of a number of songs for which he could also find the song's name to match his image. He could see the song he wanted but he couldn't find its name. I asked him to describe the picture: a hand with two fingers up. While I was guessing songs with two items, songs with the number two, anything "two," my hand (with two fingers raised) was bouncing and he got it— *Little Bunny Foo Foo!* This was a song I had not sung to him in many years, maybe four or more, but the image,

Matt's "Shelf of Songs"

the picture he had created of the song, lived on in his mind's eye, on his shelf of songs.

On another occasion, when Matt was about six, I had been summoned to his bedside for one last whisper, snuggle and butterfly kiss. In my attempt to plot a course across the four feet between the bedroom door and his bedside I had managed to plant my unprotected left foot smack on top of a Mars colony created from LEGOs™. (Who makes these things and why are they so tough on bare feet?!) As I attempted to regain my balance (and refrain from swearing out loud) my right foot landed on and collapsed the K'Nex™ version of the International Space Station. I was clearly losing the navigational battle of my child's bedroom floor. Then, on my way to greeting that when-was-the-last-time-this-was-vacuumed-floor with my face, I noticed that hurled under the bed frame, like so much forgotten dirty laundry, was the homework assignment that was *DUE THREE WEEKS AGO!!*

Of course, in your topsy-turvy world, the LEGOs™ and K'Nex™ could be replaced with puzzles, art, construction materials, books, blocks, marbles, beads, Play-Doh®, ribbons, scissors, stuffed animals, chess pieces or any number of other assorted items. And the misplaced homework could be anything else that nobody but you seems to understand the value and importance of—like, say, homework.

Here's another memorable event that defined for me how Matt thinks: One evening, after enjoying a take-out meal from a local restaurant, he couldn't wait to get his hands on some tape and the styrofoam containers our food had been delivered in. He actually "saw" airplane propellers in the lids, an airplane body in the boxes and all the other pieces required to create his custom jet. They were all there—their potential being wasted just holding our food. When dinner was over, voila, the airplane was created—food crumbs and all! (I'm almost certain it still exists somewhere, probably under his bed!) Visual-spatial kids not only see a variety of uses for everyday things, they can visualize in multiple dimensions how to transform those objects into innumerable items. Sequential thinkers would likely just throw such "junk" away.

By the way, it is extraordinarily difficult for topsy-turvy kids to give up these wonderful products of their imaginations. They form very strong attachments to whatever they create and can't bear to see anything trashed. Eventually, however, there comes a time (in our house it's not until we've got a fire hazard on our hands!) when some of these creations must meet their end. In an attempt to ward off bitter disagreements that the time has come to trash Matt's beloved diorama of

African animals or Sam's construction of an entire city's infrastructure from cardboard, we let the boys take photos of their creations to save and treasure within their own scrapbooks. This seems to lessen the pain of seeing it stacked up along the sidewalk waiting for the trash pick-up because they know they have evidence that it existed. They can each recall the fun they had building their project as they review their scrapbook, the hallways are once again clear and hazard-free (at least temporarily) and everyone is happier for having avoided possible fighting and tears.

Bear with me through one more story about identifying Matt's learning style. Once, as we were headed out for some unmemorable chore and still backing out of the driveway, Visual-Spatial Poster Child was obviously struggling in his seat. "What's up?" I called back. "I can't get the backward seven to work!" I'm thinking, *backward seven??*"—what is it? How does it work? And why does he need it? "Uh, what's a backward seven, Honey?" I cautiously asked. Meanwhile, I'm headed down the street and the panic level in his voice is rising. At the stop sign I looked back to discover that he had not been able to connect his seatbelt, which, from his vantage point, coupled with his ability to see the image and not find the matching word, was clearly a backward seven!

Are my stories of discovering Matt's learning style sounding like events from your life? Can you relate to the frustration, not to mention sore feet, of having a budding inventor/architect in your midst? How about the creation of wondrous architectural "treasures" from your trash? Well, fasten your "backward seven" (seatbelt!): it's going to be an interesting journey understanding the inner workings of your topsy-turvy children. But, trust me, it'll be worth the ride because, in the end, you'll have better communication skills to use with your visual-spatial children, be well-equipped to advocate for their needs in the classroom and be able to teach your children, as well as those who work closest with them, to honor their unique learning style.

So what does it all mean?

What I discovered about Matt's learning style (and to some extent, Sam's) is that he thinks in images. His brain is one gigantic filing system of pictures that symbolize words (like song names). Sometimes the corresponding word for the image or picture is easily retrieved but other times, the "downloading" may take awhile. His brilliant ideas take time to translate into words. To memorize material, like times tables, he must be able to create and store those facts as pictures. Then those pictures must be converted to words in order for Matt to provide an answer to your question.

When you think of a computer downloading text versus downloading images, you understand the struggle these kids face. Streams of text can be downloaded and recalled almost instantly on a computer. Images, however, can take considerably longer. For the visual-spatial child, the image is readily there, but downloading the translation of that image into something that can be communicated—the actual words to describe that picture—can be such a time-consuming struggle for them. If a picture is worth a thousand words and they are trying to communicate it in just a few, you can imagine the frustration that develops.

Visual-spatial students can often solve complex math equations accurately, but they may not always be able to show their work. For this, they are usually penalized and seldom recognized as academically talented. These kids excel in right-hemispheric strengths: art, geometry, thinking in multiple dimensions, music, creativity, empathy, design and invention, and the sheer joy of creating something wonderful out of the trash you nearly threw away. But these are talents that are often overlooked by teachers and parents in their preoccupation with grades and academic achievement. Unfortunately, because most teachers and most classrooms are sequential in nature (teaching step-by-step, details first, big picture last), children who learn in a manner compatible with that method, known as auditory-sequential learners, are often the only students recognized and rewarded for their academic performance.

Visual-Spatial Learner

Characteristics Comparison

The Auditory-Sequential Learner	The Visual-Spatial Learner
Thinks primarily in words	Thinks primarily in images
Has auditory strengths	Has visual strengths
Relates well to time	Relates well to space
Is a step-by-step learner	Is a whole-part learner
Learns by trial and error	Learns concepts all at once
Progresses sequentially from easy to difficult material	Learns complex concepts easily: Struggles with easy skills
Is an analytical thinker	Is a good synthesizer
Attends well to details	Sees the big picture; may miss details
Follows oral directions well	Reads maps well
Does well at arithmetic	Is better at math reasoning than computation
Learns phonics easily	Learns whole words easily
Can sound out spelling words	Must visualize words to spell them
Can write quickly and neatly	Much better at keyboarding than handwriting
Is well organized	Creates unique methods of organization
Can show steps of work easily	Arrives at correct solutions intuitively
Excels at rote memorization	Learns best by seeing relationships
Has good auditory short-term memory	Has good long-term visual memory
May need some repetition to reinforce learning	Learns concepts permanently; does not learn by drill and repetition
Learns well from instructions	Develops own methods of problem solving
Learns in spite of emotional reactions	Is very sensitive to teachers' attitudes
Is comfortable with one right answer	Generates unusual solutions to problems
Develops fairly evenly	Develops quite asynchronously (unevenly)
Usually maintains high grades	May have very uneven grades
Enjoys algebra and chemistry	Enjoys geometry and physics
Masters other languages in classes	Masters other languages through immersion
Is academically talented	Is creatively, technologically, mechanically, emotionally or spiritually gifted
Is an early bloomer	Is a late bloomer

Two ways of learning: auditory-sequential and visual-spatial

From **Upside-Down Brilliance**, the Characteristic Compar-
ison on the previous page lists the two general ways of
learning: auditory-sequential and visual-spatial.

Most people, I have learned, are a little sequential and a
little spatial. These abilities are not exclusive. My older son,
Sam, for example, is very strong in both auditory-sequential
abilities and visual-spatial abilities. His auditory-sequential
strengths allow him to learn well from lectures, absorbing
details like factual data, names and historical dates that he
can later accurately recall. He excels at reading, creative
writing and spelling—all traits of a strong auditory-sequential
learner. At the same time, though, he is able to "see" in multiple dimensions, can grasp complex concepts and he has a
deep appreciation for art and music—all characteristic of a
visual-spatial learner. What a gift to be able to call upon the
strengths of either or both hemispheres of the brain at any
given time.

Matt, however, must be able to create a picture of what he
is learning, literally a movie in his mind or a single image he
can draw, in order for the information to be retrieved. Math
facts memorized? Better make them funny, silly or otherwise
memorable. Dates and names recalled with accuracy? Better
have them on a timeline, full of color, with pictures to represent
events and people or use acronyms, rhymes and jingles of the
facts you want him to recall. Spelling words? They had better
have color, variation in letter size, combined with a silly
picture or some other humorous, memorable presentation, an
image that will stick in his memory. Without these visual
clues, the knowledge has no file to be placed in, no glue to
hold. This is true for most visual-spatial learners. More drill
and repetition will not work to help them retain new
information.

Have you ever taken on an art or decorating project that
you created and designed yourself? This could be anything
from a holiday craft project to completely remodeling your
living room, but it must be something you thought up and
designed on your own. Now picture that project: what exactly
did it look like? Can you see the design you created in your

mind's eye? Of course you can! You can recall that picture because you created it. You had a permanent image to retrieve from the file of pictures in your brain. Now what if I asked you to drill and repeat your picture ten times? That would be silly, wouldn't it? The image was created by you and will forever be retrievable by you. The same is true for anything your visual-spatial child learns. Drill and repetition are necessary for the left hemisphere to retain information, not the right hemisphere, the auditory-sequential learner, not the visual-spatial learner. There is no need for drill and repetition as long as your child has successfully created an image. The images are permanent.

When my sons receive a new LEGO™ set, they quickly glance at the finished product on the box, excitedly rip open one end, run for the scissors to open all the plastic bags containing their new treasures and begin assembling. Instructions? Directions? *Are you kidding?* They saw the plane, car, roller coaster, whatever, on the box. What's there to read about? They immediately understand from seeing the finished product what is required to create it. They may not follow the precise steps as outlined in the instructions, but the completed creation will mirror the photo and my children's pride in the finished piece is immeasurable.

To force either of my children to read through the step-by-step procedure: "Connect five small red rectangles to the two blue squares, blah, blah, blah," then have them actually perform those steps—*in order*—would be to alter the very way they learn, create and understand. They would quickly grow frustrated, throw the instructions on the floor and walk away. Guaranteed. A fun, challenging project just became work, work they would struggle to accomplish, fail to understand and ultimately give up on. I must remind myself that this is true for every aspect of their lives. If either of my children was forced to show his work on every math problem, to follow it to completion according to someone else's rules and steps, he couldn't do it. He would soon give up in frustration, walk away from the assignment and convince himself he wasn't able to do math at all. Not only that, he would be labeled as inattentive or unable to complete the work. His frustration might earn him various diagnoses that were inaccurate and potentially harmful.

It is important to note that the two children in the cartoon on the previous page are happy creating their project in their own way and that both will likely have a finished product very similar to the manufacturer's intention. They just completed their project in very different manners. No learning style is preferable to another. The point is to make certain we are teaching our children in whatever style they prefer.

In an effort to meet the needs of children like mine, the parents and teachers of these unique kids must first recognize that there are distinct differences in how a significant percentage of the population thinks and learns. Validation studies with the *Visual-Spatial Identifier* using middle school students revealed that **at least** one-third were strongly visual-spatial. (Please see Chapter 14 of **Upside-Down Brilliance: The Visual-Spatial Learner** for more information on the studies and results.) It is, quite simply, how these children are wired. While some visual-spatial learners may be able to adapt to another learning style, just as a left-handed person may be able to adapt and learn to use tools created for right-handers, it will never be the most efficient nor successful method for them. Many of us are strongly auditory-sequential or strongly visual-spatial, just as many of us are strongly left-handed or strongly right-handed. It's not something that can be easily altered. And, just as we no longer force left-handed children to write with their weak hand, it's time to stop asking children who rely primarily on the right hemisphere of their brain to switch to their left hemisphere to learn.

The cost of not recognizing your children's learning style

So why is it so important to understand the preferred learning style of your children? It's about effective communication. It's about reaching forward to meet these topsy-turvy kids on their terms, on their level, in their playing field. At least until they've learned the skills to play successfully in yours. It's about giving all children a chance to succeed in the classroom, to find their place utilizing their strongest talents and gifts and to use those strengths to facilitate their learning and enjoy their future careers.

Let me share a childhood experience with you about effective communication. My grandparents were both deaf, but capable of remarkably clear speech and the ability to read lips. They communicated so well that neither knew sign language. My grandmother had been taught to speak with great inflection and those who met her initially did not know that she was deaf. I would go on errands with her and she would be able to carry on small talk with the store clerk, librarian, etc. The conversation would continue until, inevitably, the clerk would turn her face away and my grandmother would no longer be able to see, *or read*, the clerk's lips. Being Grandma's Little Helper, I would pipe up with, "Oh, my grandma's deaf." Nearly every time the clerk's response was, **"PAPER OR PLASTIC?"** They would actually yell at my deaf grandmother! The only form of communication they knew, whether it was effective or not, was to raise their voice, to continue speaking to her, even with their heads turned away. The only form of communication they knew was not effective in reaching my grandmother.

If your children are VSLs and you aren't communicating with them in the manner in which they learn best, by using pictures, by helping them to create permanent images in their mind of what they are learning or of what you are asking of them, then you aren't getting through. Your communication attempts are doomed to fail. If they can't see what it is you want from them, whether it's tying their shoes, caring for the family pet or straightening their rooms, you are likely to be disappointed with the results. If there is no picture created in their mind of the math facts they must memorize or the historical dates they are to remember, they will struggle to succeed. You haven't given them the right tool for the job and you aren't communicating the way they think and learn. In order for topsy-turvy children to succeed, whether at school or at home, we, as their parents and first teachers, simply must find ways to effectively communicate with them.

With young children, I often recommend creating and using actual pictures of what you'd like done. Chore charts should feature illustrations, clip art from the computer or pictures from magazines of what the clean room, full cat food dish, brushed teeth—whatever the chore is—should actually look like when completed. Remember to use color and humor in your communications. With school-age children, ask them to repeat back to you what they believe you have asked of them. Not in a demeaning way, by any means, but as a way to confirm that your request is understood and a picture of the task at hand is accurately formed. Without the picture in mind, they are not likely to get the job done. However, with an agreed-upon image of the chore, these children stand a better chance of success.

Who Exactly are These Topsy-Turvy Kids?

I'm going to assume that you haven't clearly defined your children's unique learning style and start where all good stories should start: at the beginning. The visual-spatial learner concept comes from Dr. Linda Silverman, who coined the term in 1981. In the process of testing children's intelligence she discovered a pattern among kids who scored in the highest ranges. They did so with their phenomenal abilities to solve problems presented to them visually and by excelling in the spatial tasks of intelligence tests (e.g., Block Design, Block Counting, Rotations, Transformations and Orientation Problems). As director of the Gifted Development Center, Linda analyzed hundreds of children's test results and she saw two distinct learning styles: auditory-sequential and visual-spatial. Her theory comes down to this: We each have two hemispheres of the brain. While most of the population (roughly two-thirds) relies primarily on their left hemisphere to acquire and store new information, a significant number of people rely more on their right hemisphere. School is geared to left-hemispheric learning. Those who favor their right hemisphere are at a distinct disadvantage. Because they are presented with new material in a sequential fashion, they are required to use their weaker hemisphere, rather than their stronger. (It is important to note that both hemispheres work together to accomplish most cognitive tasks. It would be wrong and, in fact, silly, to conclude that a student is exclusively right- or left-brained, functioning with only half a brain!)

Linda's contention is that if visual-spatial learners were honored for their gifts, rather than penalized, they would flourish in academics and subsequent careers. In many ways, we all benefit from the success of VSLs. It is from the power of the right hemisphere that we enjoy elaborate musical productions, fantastic computer animations and other creations from topsy-turvy kids who were lucky enough to find careers that demand their rich imaginations and creativity.

I had the distinct opportunity to be the very first person to read the complete manuscript of **Upside-Down Brilliance: The Visual-Spatial Learner** by Linda Silverman, before it went to press. As I devoured chapter after chapter, I found myself repeating the same thought: Had Linda had been hiding within my own home? She had to have been living amongst us to know all the intimate details she wrote about! In page after page, I found not only my children, but my husband, as well. (*Hmm, I wonder where the kids got it from?*) Of course, she wasn't under the coffee table; it's just that the experiences of raising topsy-turvy kids can sound quite similar from home to home and child to child. One reader recently wrote to the Gifted Development Center website, "It was like you knew my 12-year-old son personally!" This is a sentiment I hear quite often when I travel with Linda.

Approaches to learning

Visual-spatial children approach all of their learning in a completely different manner from sequential children. The differences can be moderate to dramatic but if you're the parent of one sequential child and one spatial child, you've probably witnessed a number of distinctions. Beginning at a very young age, auditory-sequential children learn such skills as walking and riding a bike through repeated trial and error. They grab onto the couch, the table, Mom's hands, etc., and use them to pull themselves up before finally letting go and, eventually, walking unassisted. Visual-spatial children, on the other hand, may never utilize props to help them learn the art of walking. They watch intently as those around them stand and walk, learning how to perform the action by what they see. Then, one day, they just repeat what they have witnessed. This is precisely what Sam did. He was thirteen months, three days old (it was my husband's birthday so I can recall it exactly) when, after months of only crawling and with no attempt to walk while holding the couch, the coffee table or my hands, he just stood up and walked! Across the floor, down the hall, he was walking! Upright and ready to go, the boy finally walked. He had been mentally rehearsing, perfecting his balance and movement and the act of being on only two feet in his mind's eye until he finally realized he could physically perform the act of walking. In time, I would chalk this experience up to his perfectionism. It wasn't until years later that I would read **Upside-Down Brilliance** and understand that this was a function of his learning style, of being a visual-spatial learner, of having to see precisely how to perform a particular feat long before he could attempt it.

Sam approached learning to speak the same way. I actually thought for a time that he might be developmentally delayed because he didn't babble like my friends' babies. While he did not respond to me verbally, I always felt we were having conversations. I never doubted that he understood everything I said to him and I often felt I knew what he was communicating, even without any spoken words from him. Suddenly, choosing to skip the whole, "mama-dada" phase, my son went straight for the full sentences. Sam's "first word" was, "Mom! Look at that truck!" To which I responded by nearly falling off the couch!

Learning to ride a bike was the same story. (You would think my husband and I could have started predicting a pattern in Sam's learning, wouldn't you?) After weeks and months of watching the other kids in the neighborhood ride, it was finally time to remove the training wheels. Of course, we had to do this at a park, not in our own neighborhood. And it had to be very early in the morning so as not to be witnessed by anyone else—my children are very private people. I can remember my words of warning and assuring Sam that he would most certainly fall; he might even scrape a knee, but then he would get back on and we would be right there to support him. Surprisingly, he just got on that bike and rode! My husband was ready to hold the back of Sam's bicycle seat and run alongside him, but off he went while we stood there, dumbfounded.

For the visual-spatial child, to stand back and observe—sometimes over a long period of time—is to learn. As you will learn within these pages, it would be unwise to deny visual-spatial learners the time they need to process what they are watching (learning) and expect them to just start doing. They will likely become frustrated and give up altogether.

A VSL checklist to identify your children

Just in case you're still not sure if you have one of these kids, here's a checklist (on the following page) of the characteristics of visual-spatial children. If you aren't certain about a question, ask your children. If they are too young, you may try to answer for them, but I think you'll be surprised at what they are able to tell you about themselves. Most people who think in words can't possibly imagine that others are capable of thinking in pictures and vice versa. Unless you are also a visual-spatial learner, you may be very surprised to hear about how your kids think, learn and understand the world around them. On the other hand, some questions will be difficult for them to answer because most children are not quite ready to perceive these differences in themselves. If they are not able to answer a question, consider the examples that follow each characteristic and see if they fit your child.

Is Your Child a Visual-Spatial Learner?

Please complete this quiz to find out more about your child's learning style.

		Yes	No
1.	Does your child think mainly in pictures instead of in words?		
2.	Is your child good at solving puzzles or mazes?		
3.	Does your child like to build with LEGOs, K'Nex, blocks, etc.?		
4.	Does your child often lose track of time?		
5.	Does your child know things without being able to tell how or why?		
6.	Does your child remember how to get to places visited only once?		
7.	Can your child feel what others are feeling?		
8.	Does your child remember what is seen and forget what is heard?		
9.	Does your child solve problems in unusual ways?		
10.	Does your child have a vivid imagination?		
11.	Is your child talented in music, dance, art or drama?		
12.	Can your child visualize objects from different perspectives?		
13.	Is your child organizationally challenged?		
14.	Does your child love playing on the computer?		
15.	Is your child terrible at spelling?		
16.	Does your child like taking things apart to see how they work?		
17.	Does your child have at least one visual-spatial parent?		

If you answered *yes* to at least **9** of the above questions, your child is most likely a visual-spatial learner.

You need this book!

1. Does your child think mainly in pictures instead of in words?

This can be a difficult question because the way someone thinks has been the same for him or her since birth. To contemplate thinking differently is nearly unimaginable. If your children answer with a shrug of the shoulders, ask a question about something to which the answer is known but may require some thought. Maybe a math problem they can do mentally, or a spelling word they know. Watch their eyes as they contemplate their answer. A look to the upper left means the right hemisphere is being accessed, hence a visual-spatial child. A look to the upper right means the left hemisphere is being accessed, as for an auditory-sequential child. Once the answer is given, ask your children if they can look at their answer in their mind's eye. Now, is the answer a picture or a word?

2. Is your child good at solving puzzles or mazes?

We get puzzle stories from parents all the time! Sometimes visual-spatial kids mix the pieces of several different puzzles together to increase the challenge, sometimes they turn all the pieces upside-down and reassemble them with the brown side facing! Mazes are seldom a challenge as they readily see a way out. Here's one parent's story:

> I just stumbled across your website and was amazed to see my son described here. A little bit about him... by age 3, he was doing complex puzzles (100 pieces). One day he mixed three 100-piece puzzles together and proceeded to work them all at once...assembling all three at one time.

This advanced ability with puzzles is a sure clue to a visual-spatial learner. They see how pieces fit together, how to get out of a maze and how to solve three-dimensional puzzles easily.

3. Does your child like to build with LEGOs™, K'Nex™, blocks, and other construction materials?

> She will spend hours with blocks, LEGOs™, 3-D puzzles, sorting buttons, bolts, and such. Normal plastic one-action toys have no appeal.

Male or female, VSLs love to create. Whether it's with traditional building toys or creating their own, the home of a topsy-turvy child is typically cluttered with a variety of creations. I have to put my kids on a weekly ration of Scotch tape or we'd go through dozens of rolls a week! And what about graph paper? I can barely keep enough supply on hand for all the floor plans and models my boys want to create. Keep in mind, too, that as much as VSLs love to build, they also love to take apart! I haven't thrown out a broken appliance since my kids were born. Each has become a treasure in their beloved "science lab" just waiting to be taken apart, its secrets revealed. I received this e-mail from the mother of a technically minded daughter:

> You know your kid is visual-spatial when, at 20 months, she finds a set of specialized tools for maintaining grandma's wheelchair, infers their use by herself, and successfully manages to disassemble most of it, and then instructs you on how to get it reassembled when you discover her.

4. Does your child often lose track of time?

If I had a nickel for every time I've heard, "How can it be 8:00 already, it was just 7:15?" I'd be a very wealthy woman, indeed. Completely immersed in the joy of their creations, imaginative play or artistic endeavor, my sons are absolutely incapable of grasping the concept of The Passage of Time. They'll actually argue with me that I've altered the clock! Look for clues to answer this in how long play and creating will hold your children's attention. Note their temperament when asked to end an activity despite having had ample time devoted to it. Tip: To help your children actually envision the passage of time, try using an inexpensive hourglass. Set it up while they play as a timer they can glance at and note the passage of various intervals of time. After awhile, they may be able to sense when a certain amount of time has elapsed.

5. Does your child know things without being able to explain how or why?

Does your child pop up with answers to which you find yourself asking, "How on earth did she know that?" The solutions to complex problems often come to VSLs quite easily, while material that seems "easy" to auditory-sequential learners may elude the visual-spatial child. This does not mean that answers always come quickly to VSLs; remember they need time to translate their answers, most likely pictures, into words. Here is one mother's story of her topsy-turvy son:

> Even though an evaluation shows that G excels in Speech/ Language areas (grammar, concepts, vocabulary, etc.) he has Speech/Language therapy due to the fact that he is such a visual thinker that it takes him a while to translate his thoughts/feelings into words and it affects his ability to socialize with peers at times.

Another visitor to our website wrote of herself:

> Basically, when speaking, since I am continually translating from my visual thinking processes into words, I will sometimes lose a very simple word, although I can remember lots of words and make many hand gestures to try to describe it. For example, if I lose the word "horse," I might say instead, "a large four-legged animal that many people ride," while also holding my arms out to emphasize the largeness of what I mean. Sometimes I'll even lose the power of speech altogether and merely be able to gesture in the shape of the object that I wish to say.

6. Does your child remember how to get to places visited only once?

> ...If we go to a restaurant, he can draw an exact drawing of the restaurant's floor plan, weeks later. (At three years old!)

> One night, when O was about 4 years old, my husband was outside talking on the phone with a friend who lives in another city. When I explained to O why dad was busy on the phone, O asked, "Is that the friend with the blue house?" The last time we had been to see this friend was when O was 18 months old! He could also remember directions to places after only going there once, telling me, "There's where we turn to go to so and so's." On more than one occasion, we received calls from friends who lived over half a mile away telling us that our child had escaped our cul-de-sac and ridden his bicycle to their house!

" MOM, YOU JUST MISSED YOUR TURN."

Upside-Down Brilliance includes a number of anecdotes about toddlers correcting their parents' driving errors from the backseat. Their spatial perception and awareness is keen and they know when you've made a wrong turn. Taking a new route can be quite upsetting. It's almost as though they have an internal Global Positioning System wired into their brain! Again, photographic memory is at work with VSL children who are able to recall, as vivid pictures in their mind, precisely what the landscape, architecture and roads look like to places they've only seen once. One young boy's mother wrote:

> An additional hint [that he is visual-spatial] would be his hand and voice directions from the stroller pointing out the multi-turn route to the playground to the sitter. Too bad she failed to appreciate the humor in the situation!

7. Can your child feel what others are feeling?

Empathy is a very powerful tool, particularly for visual-spatial children. I've heard tales of children offering hugs and other comforts to people just out of a sense that something wasn't right. Has your child ever known, without explanation, that something was wrong? Disagreements between the adults in their lives cannot be kept from them. They are too keenly aware of emotions, too perceptive of subtle changes in behavior in those around them. It is not unusual for visual-spatial children to feel they can communicate with animals and can understand an animal's emotions, too.

> ... We were all feeding sea gulls at the beach one day. Needless to say there were dozens of birds all jockeying for position to snatch our bread. H began walking off toward a single sea gull alone. He felt sorry for him. I wondered why H wasn't paying attention to the 3 dozen or so birds that were hovering around us! He sees lone butterflies when we are viewing vast land-scapes, or can find the spider in the middle of the mulch bed.

> On the plus side, she's unusually aware of other people. She's solicitous and kind, has an eclectic circle of loyal friends, and keeps expanding it by reaching out to each year's crop of new students. She is not a leader; but she's a cohesive force in the group. Her experience with struggling, working hard, and over-coming obstacles—but not always succeeding—makes her patient and empathetic.

> For his 7th birthday, he decided to have a donation party instead of toys/gifts. Friends brought checks for a local veterans' charity.

It is also not unusual to hear tales of topsy-turvy children feeling great sadness for others' losses, particularly deaths, even of insects. My own children have been found creating burial mounds and conducting funeral ceremonies for ants and other bugs from our yard. It would be insensitive to mock or belittle such actions. Instead, try to understand their deep levels of emotion and help direct their energies toward positive and rewarding efforts. The proceeds of bake sales and lemonade stands could be sent to help protect endangered species or adopt a zoo animal and would go far to soothe the hurt soul of an empathic child.

> [My son is] too kindhearted, wears his heart on his sleeve, making it easy for mean-spirited kids to pick on.

Many of the topsy-turvy kids I've read about (from their parents' e-mails) have very large hearts and genuinely want to help others. It is inconceivable to them why someone would want to tease or taunt or intentionally hurt. Their compassion for others runs deep and they remain loyal to those they care about.

8. Does your child remember what is seen and forget what is heard?

This seems to be universally true for all visual-spatial learners, adults and kids. Virtually any type of new information— instructions, directions, etc.—is better retained when they have seen it as opposed to when they have only heard it. Visual-spatial learners often have photographic memories and should be allowed to use this skill to their advantage. I'll talk later about using pictures which are more easily stored and retrieved by visual-spatial kids to learn math facts, spelling rules and more. The opportunity to incorporate several senses when learning new material is an even more effective way for VSLs to learn. Kinesthetic, hands-on experiences enrich the learning and make it more permanent.

As you have experienced, topsy-turvy kids learn by observation. At just 20 months I discovered Sam "playing" on the computer. He had learned how to manipulate the mouse, get into a document and ask the printer to do its thing just by watching me! I wasn't intentionally teaching him, but he had been on my lap and seen the process maybe two or three times and learned it. If we were ducks, observers would say our children were "imprinted!" Today he approaches the computer as many kids of his generation do, without any trepidation or concern, fully understanding how it performs pure acts of magic.

9. Does your child solve problems in unusual ways?

Do they come up with seemingly off-the-wall solutions but ones that are at the same time viable? This is especially evident in children who insist on creating their own spelling rules or who devise unique ways to memorize their math facts. Their method may make little sense to others, but if it works for them, don't mess with it! This ability is also apparent in the way they approach challenges in everyday life. VSLs see an answer that most kids just don't. They can envision solutions without the world experience required by most of us. They may not always be the most efficient answers to a problem, but they work! Once, when Matt was out in the garage building something large (he's always out there building something, so don't ask me what it was this time!), he couldn't find the tape measure. So, he took a standard 12" ruler and some string, cut the string 12" long (so as not to waste any more than a foot), and used it, measuring end to end as he went. His father watched this for a moment and offered to find the retractable tape measure, which would have made this portion of the project so much easier, but Matt was content with his own solution.

10. Does your child have a vivid imagination?

I can spot a visual-spatial child from a mile away. The creative stories these topsy-turvy kids fashion with their toys or the elaborate and often quite animated and physical way they can recall places they've been, are telltale clues. With amazing detail, visual-spatial children can tell you the colors, shapes and textures of books they've read, places they've been to or inventions they've created—even if only in their mind. Watch how your children play with blocks, dolls, etc., and listen for the details. Ordinary objects become something altogether extraordinary in their play. Parents of visual-spatial children must maintain a constant supply of recyclable materials (paper towel and toilet paper rolls, empty film canisters, egg cartons, etc.) from which their children can build and invent. One parent I know has an entire closet dedicated to storing such materials.

C creates elaborate gifts for her sisters out of common household items. She can transform cardboard, tape, foil, and string into guitars that really play. Her homemade musical instruments are so lifelike that I have used them as props in plays and photos.

Look for a very sophisticated sense of humor in these kids and often, a very silly, playful outlook. Often their age peers don't get the puns and plays on words they enjoy so these kids are hungry for older audiences who will laugh at their jokes.

11. Is your child talented in music, dance, art or drama?

Some topsy-turvy kids and adults show an early prodigious talent in music or art, but not all. For many, it's simply an intense love of hearing and observing, not necessarily of creating, the music or art themselves. When you think about your children being artistically or musically inclined, think about their appreciation for the arts, be it music, drama, visual arts, etc., not just their ability to create.

I am also a musician and have a good ear for music. So much so that I can often hear a piece of music, once, and then play it back.

I remember as a child being very artistically creative, in painting, I learned to read music, self taught, by the time I was 5; I made up plays and performed them for whomever would watch. I was curious about EVERYTHING!

When [my son] was 10, my artist brother pointed out that my son could copy an upside down painting by drawing it upright, something that my artist brother said he could not do.

12. Can your child visualize objects from different perspectives?

She may be seeing two-dimensional illustrations and such more richly than many. She naturally dresses the backs of paper dolls, looks to draw the inside of a flower when a flower is being drawn. When an illustration has too much unrelated information on it, (think non-fiction informational illustrations) she shuts down and won't even look at it. On the other hand, she loves a richly detailed illustration of a story, and can use it to enhance her experience of a book or story.

Children who can "see" the back or other side of an object, while holding a flat one-dimensional picture of it, have the image of that object securely in their mind's eye. To be able to turn objects around, mentally, in multiple dimensions, is truly one of the gifts of being visual-spatial. (My husband recently told me that he and our children frequently discuss how they can view a scene from a perspective other than where they are positioned. Once, while we were watching a play, they were able to "see" what the audience and stage looked like from the point of view of the performer!) When asking your children about this, watch for explanations of what the non-visible side of an object looks like or details of dimensions that are not visible. If they can describe for you the back of a building or anything else that appears in a photograph, for example, you've got a visual-spatial learner. (And quite possibly, a budding architect, as well!)

13. Is your child organizationally challenged?

This may not be an easy question for kids to answer. The criterion must be determined by sequential learners because even VSL adults with absolute clutter don't consider themselves organizationally impaired—they can find anything they need at a moment's notice. Just because it *looks* like chaos to the rest of the world doesn't mean it's unorganized to them! To answer this for your children, watch how they keep their room organized without your guidance. Is the laundry lying around everywhere (clean and dirty mixed)? Are you just as likely to find LEGOs™ as forks on the floor? But, despite the clutter, are they able to locate their favorite book or toy from the mess? I must be visual-spatial to some degree because I have been known on occasion to be able to locate a single sheet from a huge pile of papers—just the sheet I am looking for at that moment!

14. Does your child love playing on the computer?

Read a computer programming manual (600 pages) at the age of ten, and then was able to write a simple program.

It seems the imagery and quick response afforded by the computer is especially attractive to visual-spatial kids. VSLs are often very interested in the inner workings of computer technology and can create shortcuts others did not envision. They can become easily lost in the imagery and graphics of today's computer games and, since they lack any sense of time in the first place, can often spend endless hours (if allowed!) in front of their computer screens. Also, many topsy-turvy kids seem to innately understand the inner workings of computers, figuring out on their own and at a very young age, how to successfully operate and manipulate them. Whenever something is awry on one of our computers and my husband isn't around, I'll turn to one of the kids before trying to fix it on my own! Do you do this? If so, your child is visual-spatial!

When answering the question from our website, "What are your child's hobbies?" one mother wrote:

Computers, computers, computers. Whether it is building, repairing, reading about, using... you name it. He basically loves any type of technology and seems to have an innate ability to know how things work.

15. Is your child terrible at spelling?

Obviously, this would only be for children old enough to be given spelling lists and writing assignments. Spelling accurately seems to be a problem for every visual-spatial adult and child who has corresponded with me! Even the adults who believe they are good spellers write to tell me so with numerous typos. Written English, with its often sense-less rules and countless exceptions, has got to be one of the greatest challenges visual-spatial learners face in their education.

He can figure things out that are wrong with the computer ... and he will sit down with a car model and not get up until the whole thing is put together, but yet he can't spell at all. It's amazing how badly he spells. He also can hardly write and does not seem to be able to write complete sentences, punctuate correctly or put his thoughts on paper.

I must admit that my over-40 husband still struggles to spell correctly and I'm considering giving up on him. Thank goodness for spell check on his computer, but even that has its limits. If spelling is an issue for your children, take heart. I've got some tips and techniques to try out in Chapter 5.

16. Does your child like taking things apart to see how they work?

It was very clear that A's strengths were understanding how objects worked. Toys with gears, LEGOs™, etc. were what he was first drawn toward. Everything was taken apart. He would create new objects from parts of dismantled objects.

My husband has always been exceedingly mechanically inclined. At age seven, he took apart the family vacuum cleaner that was destined for the dump. After cleaning it, oiling it and re-assembling it, it worked for another ten or twelve years. When he had finished the job, he even presented his mother with a bill for the work!

Topsy-turvy kids seem to intuitively understand how things work. And if they don't know, they will seek to under-stand the inner workings of nearly everything, either by reading voraciously about the subject, watching something on television about it or just diving in and taking it apart. At age three, Sam demanded to know how the refrigerator worked. I would have given too simplistic an answer, believing a signif-icant amount of discussion about Freon and such would have been over his head. (Plus, I wasn't too certain how the whole thing worked, anyway!) Luckily for him, his dad explained the entire process, in great detail and he has never forgotten.

J has always been a little terror when it comes to taking things apart. Like—taking the pins out of door hinges to see what happens when you close a door—or taking the toilet innards apart, etc. All of this was done before the age of 5. I remember my mom asking Jake once (he must have been about 5) how he knew everything he did (he has always amazed us with his knowledge of adult topics—hurting world, environment, animals, etc.) *J told her he had a camera in his head and he took pictures, stored them away and got them out when he needed them.* Not too long ago my mom asked him something and he said he didn't know—she asked him about his pictures and he told her he was out of film.

17. Does your child have at least one visual-spatial parent?

Heredity is probably the single most common cause of a child being visual-spatial. And, like many physical traits we pass to our children, if you or your spouse is a visual-spatial learner, you are likely to have at least one child with the same learning style. Did you find yourself identifying with many of the items on this checklist yourself or for your child's other parent? (If you are a visual-spatial adult, **Upside-Down Brilliance** is loaded with helpful information for you, too, especially Chapter 15.)

> My husband and I have always known A was very bright and teaching him was never difficult for us since we both love to teach in analogies and visuals. We never realized this was unusual or strange until it was time for him to go to school and he began to have the same struggles we had experienced growing up.

Adults who are involved with art, music, theater, mathematics, science, surgery, technology, architecture, photography, cartography, aeronautics, engineering, mechanics or design are very likely VSLs. (These also make excellent occupational choices for visual-spatial teens to consider!) Hopefully, your experiences as a visual-spatial learner in the classroom and other areas where VSLs typically struggle will benefit your children. Perhaps there are certain coping strategies you learned along the way that you can pass along. Maybe you learned rote material, like math facts, in a fashion that will make them easier for your children to learn as well. If you are a visual-spatial learner, try to think back on how you coped and what successful strategies you might still be using to manage in a largely sequential world. Share those tips with your children!

So, what was your first clue?

Her artwork was advanced compared with her peers. At 20
months, C drew her first "spider" people with eyes, nose,
mouth, ears, hair, eyelashes and cheeks. She even drew hands
with five fingers and feet with five toes inside shoes with bow
ties.

While it's never too late to understand your own learning
style, at what age do children start displaying telltale signs of
their own preferences? I've read anecdotes of babies as young
as ten months understanding when pictures were presented
upside-down or being attracted to mirrors and their own
faces. Early signs of a visual-spatial learner include many of
the items listed on the checklist, *Is Your Child a Visual-Spatial
Learner?* on page 17, especially vivid imagination, facility with
puzzles, mazes and drawing, building with LEGOs™, K'Nex™,
and other construction toys, and a desire to take things apart
to see how they work.

Late talking compared to siblings can be an indicator, as
well. Delayed speech means that the right hemisphere is
leading the way in your child's development and the left hemisphere may be lagging behind. Researchers from Miami
Children's Hospital studied children between the ages of two
and eight with speech delays and compared them to children
whose speech was progressing normally. By using noninvasive,
radiation-free brain scans, scientists scanned children's
brains while they were sedated and played audiotapes of their
mothers' voices. The researchers were able to note which
areas of the brain were receiving more oxygen, or being relied
upon more, while performing the task of passive listening.
They discovered that the children whose speech was
progressing normally were utilizing the left hemisphere of
their brain, while the children who were considered delayed in
their speech development were using the right hemisphere.
Since re-wiring one's brain is not an option, teaching to a
child's right-hemispheric strengths will remain the best
method for visual-spatial children to achieve success.

It is a good idea to have any speech development issues
investigated by an audiologist. It is essential to rule out auditory
impairments since it is critical that they be ameliorated early.
Keep in mind, though, that any comparative delay may just be

signs of your child's special wiring, a lifetime of creativity and all the other gifts that come with right-hemispheric strength.

Remarkable ability with puzzles at a relatively young age is another telling sign of visual-spatial talent. The most frequent response to, "When did you first notice that you or your children had unusual visual-spatial abilities?" on our website was "puzzles." In fact, it is mentioned more than any other indicator of early visual-spatial ability for both boys and girls. We've received numerous stories of children who turn the puzzle pieces right-side down, or mix several puzzles together, in order to increase the challenge. They work to reassemble the pieces based on their shape, not the picture printed on them, because they see how the pieces fit together rather than relying on the completed photograph.

Mazes are a huge passion for young visual-spatial children, too. My children discovered mazes on the backs of children's menus at various family restaurants. Before they were three years old, they could each complete a maze in astounding time. Then they started creating mazes and adding them to everything they ever wrote! Every thank you card, Christmas or birthday wish, any correspondence that came from them, included a maze for the reader to follow to get to the final sentiment.

> Completing mazes [is] one of my daughter's unique talents. The vice principal has in her office a couple of adult mazes my daughter completed when she was 6.

If, at this point, you are fairly certain that your child is a visual-spatial learner but you find that they don't have a passion for puzzles or mazes, you should probably consider whether there are visual processing issues involved. I don't mean the simple distance vision test that your pediatrician offers. Rather, are both eyes tracking together, sending a single, comprehensible image to the brain? You must visit a behavioral optometrist to accurately determine this for your children. When Matt was five, he passed the 10-foot vision-screening test that his pediatrician gave him but a machine that tracked each eye while he read caught that each of his eyes was reading a different line of text simultaneously. Because he was reading at a higher grade level than his age, neither his teacher nor I had any suspicions of reading

difficulty. Six months of vision therapy and glasses for
nearsightedness cured him of this issue.

Some parents of topsy-turvy kids have pretty incredible
stories of how they were able to identify their children's
obvious visual-spatial learning style. These are always a treat
to read and often remind me of my own children or other
topsy-turvy students I've taught. Here's a great tale from a
mother of a young topsy-turvy boy:

> At 2 and a half, G was at preschool having "show-and-tell",
> when a child pulled a small soccer ball out of a bag. The
> teacher asked him, "Do you know what that is?" He said, "A
> white sphere with black pentagons on it."

No question about it! Any kid who loves shapes so much
that he knows the names of them at just two-and-a-half years
old has got to be a visual-spatial learner! (And likely highly
gifted, as well.)

Because visual-spatial learners actually view the world differently, in the same way artists do, they are often able to express themselves artistically and through a variety of mediums early on. I've read tales of very young children able to draw their toys, animals and surroundings in great detail. Talent in the arts, whether it's drawing, painting, music or drama, or some other creative pursuit, is often admired in young children. Unfortunately, if those children are not able to match that ability by excelling in traditional academics (math, spelling, reading), their art is no longer appreciated, and they may be labeled and treated for what is "wrong with them." Their relatively mediocre performance in scholastic endeavors causes their artistic gifts to be overlooked and sometimes forgotten. These are children who feel shame and embarrassment for their failings rather than pride and self-confidence for their abilities. Is that really what we want for our children? This book was written with the hope that change is on the horizon; and that visual-spatial learners everywhere, of every age, will be honored for their gifts.

Topsy-turvy kids and milestones

If only I knew then, when my boys were babies, what I know now. Well, I didn't so the next best thing is to help others, right? If I had known about preferred learning styles and that Sam was a visual-spatial learner when he was at the age to begin walking, I wouldn't have worried about why he seemed to be lagging behind his age peers, why he wasn't pulling himself up along the couch, why he refused to hold my hands and mock the act of walking. If only I had under-stood that all that time I was worrying, he was busy studying! By watching everyone around him walk and mentally rehearsing the act himself, he was able to skip all the "normal" precursors to becoming a full-fledged walker. A watched pot doesn't boil and VSL children aren't going to graduate through prescribed milestones until they're ready, until they've mastered them mentally and are ready to spread their wings on their own timetable. If I'd known then that Sam was a visual-spatial learner and what that meant in terms of how he would learn and develop, I wouldn't have needed to be so concerned about his seemingly delayed speech, either. It wasn't delayed at all, but actually ahead of schedule by the time he uttered that first full sentence, rather than cooing and babbling any first words.

So, my point is this, if your topsy-turvy, very young kids are obviously enjoying visual stimulation like looking into mirrors, if they can recognize when a book is upside-down or they can easily assemble puzzle pieces or you have other reasons to believe they are visual-spatial learners, relax. Your children will reach those walking, talking, bike-riding milestones in their own sweet time. You will be able to relish capturing those Kodak moments, but not until your children are ready to offer them and most likely, not when your friend's children are reaching them. As your children's first teacher, make sure you are demonstrating the skills they need to learn because you can be certain they're watching. By observing how you do the simplest tasks, from safely cutting a sandwich to navigating a flight of stairs, your topsyturvy kids will learn more from your actions than they ever could from your words.

Maintaining Harmony at Home

There's no doubt about it, life with topsy-turvy kids—particularly if you are an auditory-sequential parent—can be challenging. They have no sense of time, so you're generally late getting out the door. Their organizational skills are lacking, or at best questionable, so you feel as though you are living in a giant collection of STUFF all of the time. They tend to become easily distracted, so chores and homework assignments are often not completed according to a teacher's or parent's time schedule, which can result in significant tension. So, how do you maintain harmony?

Housekeeping—it's not just a job, it's an adventure

How effectively are you communicating with your child? Imagine it's time for the weekly (monthly?) Clean-Your-Bedroom-Or-Else Ritual. Do you typically rattle off a list of do-this, do-that chores then leave the room believing that your "picture" of a clean living space will somehow manifest itself out of the reigning chaos? And, that it will do so within a prescribed timeframe? Now think about your success rate with this approach. (Not great, I'm guessing!) Next time, try this: work with your child to create a poster or chart of pictures (e.g., drawings you create together, clip art from the computer, photographs or clippings from magazines, etc.) of what the end product, the Never-Been-Seen-Since-We-Moved-In-Bedroom, should look like when the job is finished. The pictures might include one of a nicely made bed with all the stuffed animals aligned. Another picture could show folded clothes neatly tucked into drawers that are still within the dresser, while another picture might show matching shoes lined up nicely on the floor of the closet. Yet another image of similar toys gathered carefully into tubs ... OK, you get the picture. Now help them get the picture.

One clever mother shared with me that after she and her daughter were successful in creating a perfectly clean and orderly bedroom that both parent and child could live with, they took a photo of it to use as a reminder of the goal the next time the bedroom got out of hand.

I believe all children, not just visual-spatial learners, should be involved in helping to maintain the home from an early age. Not only because scrubbing floors and the ability to do one's own laundry are strong life skills, but because actually participating in the dusting, vacuuming, dishwashing and so on, develops a sense of pride and ownership. I've seen with my children that they are more likely to keep a floor clutter-free or a kitchen table cleared if they were involved in restoring it to a cleaner state in the first place. There's nothing like securing an image of what the table, room or floor should look like than to participate in getting it to that condition!

Getting them out the door—with their shoes!

Getting a visual-spatial child out the door can be a daily challenge. There are so many distracting and more entertaining options available. One technique that works, at least some of

Auditory-Sequential Learner   Visual-Spatial Learner

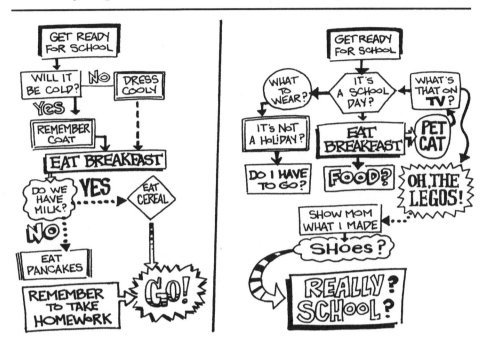

the time, is to create a mental picture of the consequences of
not getting to your destination on time. For example, suppose
you are running late to an afternoon sports practice. You could
create the following picture for your child: "If we are late for
your practice, that will upset the coach and possibly interrupt
the start of the practice for all the other kids who arrived on
time. How do think your coach will feel? How will the other kids
feel?" If they can envision the experience and understand the
consequences of not arriving on time, you may actually stand a
chance of getting out the door—and, possibly even with their
shoes! I have actually had one of my children (who shall remain
unnamed) arrive at our not-so-close-to-home destination and
ask, "Where are my shoes?" to which I replied, "ON YOUR
FEET, *right*?" They weren't and we wound up searching for the
nearest Target store!

Assure your children that whatever they were longing to do instead of getting in the car will be there for them when they return. Visualizing what will happen, or not happen, as a result of their action, or inaction, is often a successful way to get results. Also, effective although militaristic sounding, are one word commands: "Shoes-Car-Please" convey all the instructions they need. Not much decoding is required!

One parent wrote me with a great idea for helping her son to get ready on time, every morning. They sat down together and agreed on the chores that needed to be completed, and in what order. Then, they color-coded those chores: Blue (1) Eat breakfast, Red (2) Get dressed, Yellow (3) Brush teeth, and so on. Each morning, she would hand her son his set of cards, each with Velcro tabs, which he would take with him to each task and stick them to the dresser, mirror, etc., wherever the chore had taken place. He quickly learned the morning routine and was able to complete the chores, without distraction, in time for them to leave for school each day.

Make it fun so the job gets done!

The right hemisphere enjoys absurdity and thrives on humor. (See Chapter 2 of **Upside-Down Brilliance: The Visual-Spatial Learner** for more on this.) So, use it everywhere! A silly, singsong voice or foreign accent engages visual-spatial children and gets them participating. In our home, we try to present chores that need doing, or some other task they dread, in a British or Australian accent. Pretty soon, the kids are mocking the accent as they complete the task. Everyone is silly about it, but the job gets done. Background music and lots of dancing work great, too! Vacuuming isn't such toil with The Beatles blaring in the background. Make daily routines a big production! What's big and fun and noisy can make chores and other dreaded rituals much less drudgery. Even Mary Poppins understood the importance of song and silliness to "help the medicine go down" or tidy the nursery!

Recently, my dear friend and her husband were stranded in a snowstorm and had to seek refuge in our home. We had about 45 minutes notice to clean house, make a fresh bed and scrub the bathrooms! We gobbled down the rest of our dinner and set to work. With the radio blaring, we each set to a different chore. By the time our guests had arrived, not only was the house clean, but the boys had also constructed a "check-in" desk out of a cardboard box, complete with paper computer and mouse, door keys to slide into paper "locks" on their door, a welcome basket of fruit waiting in their room and room service options available for them! We had such fun anticipating their arrival that the chore of cleaning and preparing the house in a big hurry was just another necessary step in all the fun.

Oil and water? Visual-spatials and auditory-sequentials under one roof

You know your spouse isn't visual-spatial when... You have to wait for him by the salad bar, because he wouldn't be able to find his way back to the table by himself.

It is possible, although unlikely, that your topsy-turvy
children are unique in your family, that they did not inherit
their learning style from either parent; or perhaps they have a
visual-spatial parent who learned to repress a preferred
learning style in order to cope with auditory-sequential classrooms; or perhaps your topsy-turvy children were adopted
(many Asian-born children are visual-spatial). If you are not a
visual-spatial learner and your children are, you must try to
"see" from their perspective. A visual-spatial mother of two
topsy-turvy children wrote:

> You cleared up quite a bit of confusion in our family, because
> now "dad", who is only mildly visual-spatial, has an instruction
> manual for the rest of us.

If you are an auditory-sequential learner and your
children are visual-spatial learners, you will have to learn,
likely through trial and error, the most effective ways to
maintain harmony in your home.

Auditory-sequential adults often see visual-spatial
children as impulsive in their reactions. Anger or frustration
can seem to overtake them in an instant and cause them to
behave like Hyde—Jekyll's dark side. Because they are less
capable of foreseeing the consequences of their actions and
reactions and are unlikely to predict that a sequence of events
will lead to a particular outcome, (like being grounded for
hitting their brother) they may respond to various predica-
ments in inappropriate ways. For example, recently Matt has
discovered several choice foul words with which to pepper his
vocabulary. (Did I mention he recently returned to traditional
school? *Hmm.*) Because he is incapable of predicting the
responses his father and I will have to these utterances, he is
blurting them out in our presence, during moments of
extreme frustration.

An auditory-sequential child might still season his words
but probably only among his friends, when there is little risk
of repercussion. An auditory-sequential child would be able to
envision the consequences of his behavior and create alternative responses to his frustration in front of his parents. Matt,
however, has little or no means with which to calm himself,
gain some control and manage his anger. Instead, he has
added a parent's fury to the fire and now must contend with

a whole host of issues unrelated to his initial frustration. The challenge for me and my husband, as his parents, is to not react to the expression of Matt's anger, but get to the root of the frustration: what is it that caused the violent outburst, the foul language, the physical aggression or the lack of control in the first place. We'll deal with the actual words used later! (In our home, disagreeable vocabulary is tolerated to a point, so long as it is not used to hurt someone. They are, after all, just words.)

After the incident, I'll ask my son if he was so frustrated he couldn't think of a more acceptable utterance and we sometimes wind up laughing over a Thesaurus! We also have a punishment in place known as the "fine jar," or, as I prefer, Mom's Scrapbook Fund. An over-the-top blowup or meltdown results in a 25 cent fine. This goes for adults and children alike. I believe my husband may, in fact, be the largest contributor to date!

Another technique I've discovered to halt the negative responses coming from an extremely frustrated child is to get out the camera. Sounds terrible, I know! Who wants to photograph for posterity your darling child ready to hurl something at his sibling or strike a blow at him, right? But it works! The moment they realize they are about to be the subject of a scrapbook page (one of my favorite hobbies), the action stops. It takes awhile to cool down and be able to laugh at what Mom almost caught on camera but it can turn even the ugliest of arguments into play. You can actually feel the mood of the room change as the frustration dissipates and the camera hams emerge in all their silliness and goofy smiles.

Learning by watching

Imagine you are helping your visual-spatial child to master something new. OK, I'm sounding like a broken record, but whether it's riding a bike or memorizing their multiplication tables, the greatest gift you can give your topsy-turvy children is to present that new material visually. Let them watch how a particular skill, such as riding a bike, is mastered. Help them create images in their minds of how to physically accomplish a new task. Allow them the time they need to see themselves accomplish this new feat and do not place your own timetable, or anybody else's expectations, on them. A mother of one topsy-turvy boy wrote:

> When G was two, instead of running up to the bubble wand and blowing bubbles like all of his other peers...he stood back from it, observed how it worked and only when there was no pressure on him, approached it and tried blowing a bubble for himself. When G was three, he didn't play with a piñata at a birthday party until he'd observed the other children, how the piñata was played with, etc. Once the other children were done and there was no pressure on him, he approached the piñata and whacked at it a few times.

An artist cannot be rushed. Neither, then, can the visual-spatial learner. The image will be created but only on the child's terms and timeframe.

I've heard many stories of children who were quite frightened to go down a flight of stairs. I believe it's because they can easily envision the dangers and they are able to visualize the consequences of not performing it successfully. My own children never required a fence or gate at the top of the stairs; they were too afraid to get too close! Once visual-spatial learners can see in their mind's eye how they will manage the flight of stairs, the bicycle, roller-skating, even walking, then they can attempt it physically.

What is it about sleep?

What happened to all that promised naptime during babyhood? I distinctly recall reading, in more than one of those magazines for new parents, that my alone time, my time to get the laundry folded, dinner made and all the other household chores that had piled up while I was feeding them and changing diapers, would find time for completion during the Baby's Daily Nap. Some babies even napped more than once a day! *Did somebody forget to tell my children?* They came into the world with their batteries charged and rarin' to go! Maybe since these kids learn by watching, they can't afford to waste time closing their eyes?

How is it possible that no matter how active the day or how exciting the adventures, topsy-turvy children need FAR less sleep than do the adults in their lives? Even when compared to other children, it seems visual-spatial kids are more active at night. I'm an eight-hour-of-sleep-a-night mom, minimum, no matter what. More, if I've been chasing the kids around all day. My boys, however, require far less sleep to feel refreshed and ready for another round of adventure. Do visual-spatial children see all the possibilities a new day holds and can't wait for them to happen? Actually, when you think about it, what a wonderful way to greet each day, even if you haven't had all the sleep you thought you needed. (I must confess to being quite spoiled, however, because my VSL husband pulls the night duty and seemingly needs as little sleep as our boys do.)

The bedtime ritual: A recurring nightmare or the day's dreamy ending?

Do your topsy-turvy kids struggle to get ready for bed? Try making up silly songs about getting changed into pajamas, brushing teeth and any other related chores. A parent who contributed to **Upside-Down Brilliance** shared her special command: "Jambruwash" for pa**jam**as, **bru**sh and **wash** as the bedtime ritual her children were to follow. Remember, make it silly, make it fun and you've made it memorable. Making it memorable means you stand a better chance of success in seeing the task accomplished. Always remind yourself, "Do they have the picture of what I'm asking them to do?" If you've created a picture in their minds, you'll be amazed at the results.

Few things seem more conducive to stirring the imagination than lying in the dark. Besides, the end of the day is a chance to wallow in the right hemisphere, particularly if school and other demands have forced the VSL child to focus on the left hemisphere all day. Typically, while I'm envisioning my children blissfully drifting off to sleep at the end of a heavily scheduled day, they're almost always wide awake, mentally creating outrageous inventions, worrying about expectations for the next day or imagining horrible creatures behind closet doors. Remember, the topsy-turvy kid has an abundantly overactive imagination and the incomparable ability to visualize creatures out of any shadow, noise or stirring. To calm Sam when he was young and soothe him to sleep, I used to offer relaxing massages, especially to his face. I would sing or have background music playing while I gently stroked his eyelids. This seemed to help keep all frightening thoughts at bay; all worries and concerns could wait until morning. Now that he's older, he has his own methods for ensuring peaceful dreams and sound sleep. They include soothing music to drift off to, making sure the closet doors are closed and confirming all moving shadows really are just trees blowing in the breeze.

Sometimes the imaginations of topsy-turvy kids continue even while they sleep. Both of my children have been prone to horrific nightmares their whole lives. A visual-spatial woman shares her experiences with dreams:

> My dreams are vivid; as if the event had just happened, these dreams can be positive or negative. Both elicit strong emotional responses.

If your children are deep sleepers, the nightmares can be so realistic they have difficulty shaking them from their memory during waking hours. When Sam was very young, I created "Bad Dream Spray" to prevent nightmares from ever happening. I took a standard spray bottle from the grocery store, filled it with water and just a touch of blue food coloring. I would spray all around his room, especially under his bed and in his closet. He was convinced this would keep all bad dreams away and so, it did! (You have to make sure you use only a very small amount of food coloring or you'll have a bigger problem than nightmares on your hands!)

You could also use a dream catcher and hang it above your child's bed. Native American legend says that dream catchers, which have been used for generations, sift through the sleeping person's dreams, catching those that are good and sending the bad dreams through the hole in the center.

Here's another suggestion for more harmonious evenings, at least with school age and older children: we have asked our children to understand and respect that Mom and Dad just need time to be alone. The boys may not feel sleepy, but there are discussions to be had that don't concern them or TV shows to watch that are inappropriate, etc., and they'll have to entertain themselves quietly, separately and in their own rooms. Often, they just read themselves to sleep. It doesn't work every night, but it does grant us some time alone and the boys learn to quietly entertain themselves without our involvement.

Dr. Deirdre Lovecky of Gifted Resources of New England wrote with these ideas for getting kids to bed (D. Lovecky, personal communication, July 15, 2004):

> It helps to have a regular sleep schedule, in which they get up and go to bed at approximately the same time every day.
>
> Refrain from computer, video or television time within 2 hours of bedtime; research indicates that the pineal gland gets stimulated by the screen, reducing melatonin production (which facilitates sleep).
>
> Institute a bedtime routine, gradually reducing activity level. (Do not remove this routine as punishment.) A bath, a story, meditative or prayer activity, deep breathing, visualizing happy images, soft music or children's sleep tapes and relaxation activities all can be helpful in inducing sleep.

Some topsy-turvy kids are just wired for nighttime living. They are true night owls who simply don't function well during daylight hours. One parent wrote to our website that her children were "allergic to morning." I've even heard stories of families who homeschool at night because the parents and kids were all night owls!

> She will stay up to all hours watching movies or working on one of her craft/art projects. She is definitely NOT a morning person.

I have some good news for all you sleep-deprived parents: It gets better as they get older. As our children grew, they didn't need to wake us up for their needs or to entertain them. At age nine, Sam started to prepare his own break-fast—even healthy scrambled eggs or a complicated omelet. For a long time, we told our kids that, unless they were sick, they absolutely could not leave their rooms until 6:30 in the morning. They could read, play with toys or otherwise entertain themselves if they could not get back to sleep, but under no circumstances were they to play with each other (that would quickly get too loud and wake us) or wake a parent until after 6:30am—especially on weekends!

Agreed-upon visual images—a key to harmony

Unless you have created a picture for the visual-spatial learner to act on or remember, consider your request or the new material they have learned, lost. You could deliver an entire set of instructions regarding the daily care of the family pet: fill the water bowl, make sure there is enough food in the dish, check the litter box, etc., but if you have not planted the image of the chore's goal—a fed and cared for pet—your topsy-turvy child will be stuck envisioning filling the water bowl in a room full of temptations that draw attention completely away from the chore at hand. Once you think you've helped create a picture in your child's mind of what you'd like done, ask your child to describe for you what that image is.

Make sure you both agree on the "picture" that will result when the chore is complete and you're more likely to be satisfied with the end results.

The Topsy-Turvy Kid and Education

Learning thousands of years ago must have been heaven for topsy-turvy children. Each day sons and daughters spent their days with their mothers, fathers and other extended family members learning survival skills by **watching** the fine art of basket weaving; by **observing** how to select the edible berries from the poisonous ones; and having **demonstrated** for them how to successfully hunt large mammals, create warm shelter and skin animal hides for clothing. The very survival of the species depended on one generation *visually* demonstrating their set of learned skills to the next generation. Learning by observation is one of the most effective ways for visual-spatial children to truly grasp new concepts. Once a picture has been created in their mind's eye, they can recall it in specific detail, time and again. That's how so many learned behaviors were handed down for generations.

Your children's first teacher: You!

As the first teacher for your children and, likely, the first person to notice any specific learning style they may prefer, you have the unique ability to fully understand what makes them tick. You will not be able to alter this about them; it is fundamental to who they are. But you can help them learn to use their visual-spatial abilities to their advantage, as a strength to be called upon. In addition to teaching your children to honor one another for unique characteristics and abilities, you can teach your children to respect and honor their own gifts.

All parents want their children to succeed, in school and beyond. By understanding and honoring, not trying to change or "correct," how your children respond to their environment, how they think and learn best, you can help make success a reality for them. Become your children's best advocate—nobody knows them better! Advocate for them by educating their teachers about their learning style. Seek out the best educational environment for your children; don't just rely on the easiest or conventional route. What is "best" for your neighbor may be inappropriate for your child. If this approach is insufficient, consider afterschooling them (enriching what they are learning in the classroom with visual activities at home designed to increase their comprehension and retention); homeschooling them; finding a tutor or private school; or whatever else it takes. Help them find academic success using the gifts they were born with; rather than try to make them fit where they don't belong. Square pegs never fit well in round holes.

Advocating for your topsy-turvy kids

If your children are visual-spatial learners, one of your jobs as a parent is to work with your children's teachers and help them understand this preferred learning style. Chances are your children aren't the only visual-spatial learners in the classroom; studies have shown that **at least** one-third of the population is strongly visual-spatial. Another significant percentage of students who are both auditory-sequential and visual-spatial lean more toward being visual-spatial than auditory-sequential. By enriching the learning experience with a more visual, hands-on approach, with activities that engage all students, the classroom teacher doesn't sacrifice anyone's learning, nor is any one style favored over another. Enriched activities for visual-spatial learners serve to **add** to every student's learning experience. I've never met an auditory-sequential learner who didn't enjoy squishing and shaping clay to re-create ancient artifacts, but I've known several visual-spatial learners who couldn't recite the historical dates or names if they had only learned that information by reading it or hearing it in a lecture.

Today's teachers face classroom challenges unheard of in past generations. From medical diagnoses that didn't have names 20 years ago, to social and family issues that are far more rampant than they were in the past, the teachers of today's children have greater roles to play than ever before. With great empathy for teachers, I am not proposing yet another teaching theory they must master or drastic accommodations they must incorporate into their daily planners. What I am proposing, however, is this:

- That each child be honored for preferring one of two learning styles: visual-spatial or auditory-sequential.

- That the curriculum be supplemented with hands-on, visual activities that meet the needs of the visual-spatial children in the classroom and enrich the learning experience for all.

As the parent of visual-spatial children, plan to meet and discuss known preferred learning styles with your children's teachers early in the school year. Offer to help create materials that make the learning more visual and hands-on. In the early grades, this could mean folder games that reinforce specific concepts in language, math or social studies; or it could include working with all students, visual-spatial and auditory-sequential, to create silly stories for their spelling words that use color and characters in a picture of how each word is spelled or making up a silly song to remember new material. In the older grades, this could mean helping students develop organizational skills by color-coding homework, helping them to master their multiplication tables by creating humorous cartoons and remembering higher level vocabulary by using color and humor to secure definitions in their memories. (See Chapter 5 for more information on helping your children with organization skills, homework and more.)

All of these techniques will make learning more permanent for the visual-spatial learners, while enhancing learning opportunities for the auditory-sequential students. A recipe for success that few teachers could argue with! As students grow older, they can be asked to create for themselves the materials they need to help them succeed in the classroom and make their learning permanent. Matt knows that when he is given a new list of spelling words, he'd better create visual images for them because the teacher's methods (write them, cover them and write them again) don't secure them in his memory. He also knows, at age nine, that if he needs to be able to recall specific dates or names that he has read, he must create drawings (his "notes") for the information to be remembered. Whatever tricks your visual-spatial children find that work, reinforce those practices until they become habit.

When Matt was enrolled in a World History class in which he was expected to take detailed notes from the teacher's lectures, he actually took his notes in the form of drawings. He quickly drew the images that came to him from the teacher's words. At one point he was accused of simply doodling and not really paying attention. The teacher ridiculed him, showing his drawings to the class saying, "I hope the rest of you are paying better attention." Matt responded, respectfully, that he be quizzed on the material. He was and he passed. His drawings had created permanent images in his mind of all the material: the dates, names and places. He had devised his own unique way of incorporating the important dates to be recalled by using those numbers to decorate boats, landscapes and other relevant drawings. By illustrating the material, he could learn and accurately recall the historical facts. Matt passed that impromptu quiz and from then on, his teacher allowed him to take his notes in pictures and he did not question Matt's focus or attention.

> His notes from school are filled with cartoons and doodles, and one time came home with four pages of design for a robotic dinosaur museum display, complete with cross sections showing the layers of mechanical parts overlapped with muscles and rubber skin, as well as instructions on how to assemble the whole thing. (This was another one of those "what weren't you doing in school while you were doing this?" moments.)

❧ ❧ ❧

> In lectures I always took notes and drew diagrams, then never needed to look at them again.

A twist on this technique may be to ask if lectures may be tape recorded so that the student can create drawings later, after class. By doing so after the lecture, color and other helpful imagery can be added because there is no time limitation. When a lecture has been recorded, it can be stopped and replayed as needed for accuracy. This worked especially well for one VSL adult who wrote:

> ...My first year in college, I suddenly was having difficulty following lectures and taking notes at the same time. I tried buying lecture notes, but this did not always help me. Suddenly what worked for me in high school did not work for me in college. I struggled for two years not knowing why and wondering if I should even be there, until someone suggested I take a tape recorder to class. I tried it and found that when I would replay the tapes and transcribe everything down in my own hand, I began to get it. My grades went back up and I knew I had found my way to study. Since then I have found that it helps for me to make flow charts and outlines in different colored ink. If I can see it on the page, and I have the complete information, then I usually get it. But, just as you described, I have noticed that in my day-to-day dealings, I will often miss the details.

By incorporating activities that utilize the strengths of the right hemisphere: color, humor, imagery and visualization, as well as hands-on creations, you and your children's teachers will be assisting these topsy-turvy kids to successfully harness their gifts and enjoy academic success, perhaps for the first time in their school careers.

It's not that easy bein' green

I remember very clearly when I was in elementary school, coming home crying to my mother for giving me her red hair. Every day I was teased because I was different than the other kids: "Carrot-top," "Raggedy Ann," or my least favorite, "I'd rather be dead, than red in the head." As Kermit the Frog sang, "It's not that easy bein' green." And it's not easy to be different from your classmates. Distinctions in appearance or ability at a young age that are obvious to one's peers can make a child the target of bullying or teasing and dramatically affect a child's self-esteem.

From a 17-year-old female visual-spatial learner:

After reading Upside-Down Brilliance, I felt like Spider Man,
able to be a Super Hero but also bearing the curse that went
with it. I felt that I was aware of incredible strengths that go
with visual-spatial learning, but also aware of the difficulties
that kept me from being "normal."

So how do we prevent all this from happening? How do we
educate the people in our children's lives about learning
styles and honoring the distinctions in different children? Like
the solution to many of society's problems, the answer starts
at home. It has been said that children acquire more new
knowledge in the first three years of life than during any other
three-year period. The skills of crawling, walking, talking,
eating, recognizing faces, colors, numbers and letters,
decoding facial expressions and other body language, and so
much more, are all mastered in those first years. Years when
our children are doing tremendous amounts of learning at
home, from parents, not in a traditional classroom. If we, as
teacher-parents, incorporate true respect for the differences
among people, perhaps we can come closer to creating a
world that is more accepting, more tolerant, more loving and
more secure. A tolerance not just for children who learn
differently, but also for those who look differently, have an
alternative lifestyle, or stand out in any way.

Developing self-confidence in your topsy-turvy child

It is important to understand that each of us is not
completely auditory-sequential or completely visual-spatial.
We are each, to some degree, a unique blend of both learning
styles, having been born with both a right and left hemisphere that are, barring defect or serious injury, properly
connected to each other and functioning well. Those among
us who are extremely auditory-sequential (relying mostly on
the left hemisphere) are easy to spot: they tend to do well in
school, take verbal instructions and complete requests
accurately, develop their skills fairly evenly according to a
predictable timetable and are generally well-organized, with
neat handwriting and good spelling. They are early bloomers
who like to please their teachers. Most educators are

auditory-sequential (perhaps they were drawn to their profession by their own classroom success?) and enjoy how effortlessly bright auditory-sequential children think and learn. These students require very few modifications to the structure and presentation of typical curricula.

Visual-spatial learners, those who are relying primarily on the right hemisphere of their brain, on the other hand, aren't anything like their auditory-sequential counterparts. They have their own unique way of seeing the world, of inventing wonderful creations, of living entirely in the moment with no sense of time or deadlines, of seeing the whole, big, glorious picture—the forest as it were—despite the trees. They require a different set of tools to successfully communicate with them. If they don't receive those accommodations, they can feel dumb in classroom situations, frustrated that their needs aren't met at school or home, and unhappy about their uniqueness.

Some topsy-turvy children, by the very nature of being different from their peers, suffer from low self-esteem. Reassure your children that they have tremendous gifts and skills of great value. They will no doubt feel that they get smarter as they get older, something many VSL adults have reported on our website. With a clear understanding of their own strengths and weaknesses, they can face their challenges and feel adequately prepared to manage their education well. Each accomplishment will help to increase their self-confidence. This is a time for visual-spatial learners to shine because the skills they naturally possess are the ones we will continue to rely on more and more in this Computer Age. (See Chapter 7 for ideas on the future for visual-spatial learners.)

The topsy-turvy kid in school, traditionally a right-side up environment

As a homeschooling mom, I had the luxury of creating a classroom that was custom-designed to meet the unique needs of my children and their abilities. But most of what I learned in communicating with my children as their teacher was applicable to my role as their parent and it may help you, too. Whenever we approached any new material, we brainstormed about how to present it *visually*. Often my children came up with remarkably effective, visual ways they would like to learn new material. From maps of South America in multiple colors of clay (including transparency overlays of the ancient Aztec, Mayan, and Incan civilizations) to gigantic sheets of butcher paper (to trace the paths of the first Polynesian explorers and Lewis and Clark), we always incorporated some interesting visual activity to accompany and expand upon our traditional curriculum. We weren't finished truly appreciating a Shakespeare play until we had dissected it, diagrammed it and created a cartoon version of it!

Classroom use of "props" that tap into the strengths of the right hemisphere serve to enhance the overall educational experience for every learner, visual-spatial and auditory-sequential. These include math manipulatives, graphic organizers, the computer, paper, crayons and tape, colored clay, overhead transparencies and cartoons, as well as songs, dramatic gestures, rhymes, alliterations, useful acronyms, exaggerated accents, and anything else the students find humorous and memorable. Visual-spatial children remember what they see, but not always what they hear. For the information that they hear, they must be allowed time to create a visual image to accompany that new knowledge or it is lost.

Visual imagery to secure new information

I once met an incredibly dynamic teacher and conference presenter named Jon Pearson (www.createlearning.com) who taught the 13 colonies by having his audience memorize a ridiculous story—in pictures that participants created in their minds—of a Jersey cow named Georgia, atop the Empire State Building. Are you "seeing" New Jersey, Georgia and New York here? The tale went on to include all 13 colonies and after each line the audience was instructed to create an image in our mind's eye while we repeated the line back to him:

A cow named ***Georgia*** (Georgia)
It's a ***Jersey*** cow (New Jersey)
She's sitting on top of the ***Empire State*** Building (New York)

She's singing a couple of Christmas **carols** (North and
South Carolina)
Under her arm is a **Virginia ham** (Virginia and New
Hampshire)
The cow is wearing a pair of yellow **underwear** (Rhymes
with Delaware)
In its hoof is a **pencil** (Pennsylvania)
The cow is making a **Connect**-the-dots drawing
(Connecticut)
Of **Marilyn** Monroe (Maryland)
Walking down a **road** (Rhode Island)
Going to **mass** (Massachusetts)

When Jon was done, every member of the audience could
accurately recall the ridiculous images each had mentally
created and, hence, all 13 colonies. The best part is that you
don't have to be an artist to accomplish this. If you want the
images drawn, not just imagined, stick figures work just fine.
As long as the story is silly and funny and you use color,
exaggerated sizes and humor to convey the new material, it
will be remembered. You can use this trick to remember so
many different types of material, from historical data to
science principles and so much more. Why do you suppose
beginning piano students are taught the notes of the scale
Every Good Boy Does Fine? Because it works to stick in the
child's mind. Why did we learn the letters of the alphabet to
the tune of *Twinkle, Twinkle Little Star*? Because catchy tunes
serve as an anchor and they make new information permanent
and retrievable.

Humor engages the right hemisphere and helps new knowledge to stick permanently. Make it silly and they'll never forget it. I taught my sons their times tables by reading them the silliest cartoons that exchanged the names of numbers for rhyming characters and other objects. What's 8 x 2? "Skate times shoe = Sick Queen, Sixteen!" This, from the cartoon story of a queen spinning dizzily while wearing a shoe on one foot and a skate on the other until she became a Sick Queen, or "sixteen." Eventually the rhyming words were replaced altogether with the numbers they represented and the images—the math facts—stuck. (You can find the entire collection in a book titled **Memorize in Minutes: The Times Tables**, available from www.multiplication.com.) This kind of silly imagery helps the facts to be memorized and recalled.

Things that seem easy to most of us are usually of a sequential nature, precisely the weak point in a visual-spatial learner's mind. This would include learning basic math facts or spelling rules. At the same time, those things that may seem challenging to most auditory-sequential learners are usually of a complex nature requiring one to view them from multiple aspects or even dimensions. This would include complex math equations, architecture, scientific principles, choreography, composing elaborate musical scores and more—concepts that come seemingly with ease to the visual-spatial learner. A visual-spatial woman wrote:

> I am a wholistic learner. I need to see the big picture before being able to focus on the specific detail. When subjects are taught sequentially, I become very restless and impatient and unable to focus. It is only when I visualize the objective that I then see how the specific details fit into place and give them the attention they require.

Topsy-turvy kids have an innate ability to visualize elaborate systems in multiple dimensions. It's the challenge of mastering sequences of information or steps to solve problems that eludes them.

> I train horses as a hobby, and my husband will yell instructions for me to do, and I have extreme difficulty following them. I have to stop and discuss with him what he is trying to achieve and then the steps I need to take in order to get there in order to do what he needs me to do.

In order to proceed with successful learning, the visual-spatial learner must be able to visualize precisely how the parts are related to the whole, how the details form the big picture. Even before those parts and details are learned, they must be shown the overall purpose and structure or they cannot master them. This is why memorizing rote material, like times tables, is so challenging. My eldest son, Sam, has been capable of higher level mathematics for years, but for a long time, he could not quickly and accurately rattle off multiplication answers and was often found using his fingers to subtract. Matt, my youngest, however, being more strongly visual-spatial, can quickly recall the silly stories we used to memorize the math facts and his translation time (the time he needs to turn the picture into words, or numbers) has decreased dramatically.

To auditory-sequential learners, it may seem as though VSLs learn backwards: understanding the whole, then mastering the parts, rather than fully understanding the parts in order to grasp the whole. If learning new material is done step-by-step, each step building on the previous one, but with no clear understanding of the big picture, your topsy-turvy child will struggle to master the material because the meaning of each isolated fact remains unclear. For example, let's take a look at learning about adding fractions. If the lesson were to start with the mathematically correct way to combine fractions by just writing fraction equations on the board and discussing various rules about common denominators, etc., the VSLs in the class would quickly be distracted by thoughts of how soon that lesson was ending! Numbers and equations and rules with no purpose to support them, no image to create from them, are useless. If, however, they could begin with a cake or a pizza and watch it being divided and added together and understand by *seeing* that as the denominator changed to a lower number it equaled a larger piece, then the lesson would have meaning and imagery and something they could envision, an image they could easily recall. Students can literally see why it would be important to understand the rules surrounding the adding, subtracting and multiplying of fractions. They can create pictures in their minds of how to apply those rules and can succeed in that lesson. The learning will have become permanent because of the images used.

Phonics is often a struggle for visual-spatial learners. The premise behind learning to read phonetically is that the student learns very small parts that gradually build to a whole. Each small step builds upon the last until the student is blending sounds to create words. This reading method is just the opposite of how topsy-turvy kids learn best. It goes against the visual-spatial learner's preference for understanding the big picture first, then mastering the parts. Visual-spatial children who are exposed only to phonics often shy away from learning to read altogether. Reading should be taught to these kids as a whole word approach, as I'll discuss in detail in Chapter 5, Succeeding as a Visual-Spatial in an Auditory-Sequential Classroom.

> Trying to teach him to read through phonics was a total waste of time. He loved sight words. It was so weird, because he went from not reading to reading almost overnight during the summer between kindergarten and first grade.

Because visual-spatial learners thrive on challenge and understand the more complex, big picture first, they must be given sufficiently challenging material at all levels of their academic careers. Meaningful, higher level learning engages the right hemisphere. If the information being presented to your child is too slow or boring, the right hemisphere drifts off to other, more exciting and adventurous activities. You've probably seen this happen! The lights are on but nobody is home. The right hemisphere has left the building—it has literally checked out of the lesson or homework assignment. With the right hemisphere on a lunch break, the visual-spatial learner, the student who relies primarily on that portion of the brain to acquire knowledge, can do no significant learning. Whatever the discussion or workload, it should be taken to the highest level so that visual-spatial children can actively engage and participate, learn and remember.

Most curricula are designed in a cyclical fashion so that what students learn in first grade, they visit again in fourth and then in eighth or maybe high school. Each time, they may learn higher level vocabulary or more complex details, but they are studying the same subject. Because VSLs thrive on challenge, they can often go straight to the more challenging material and master it at an earlier grade. Back when Sam was in first grade, his class was studying Ancient Egypt. His teacher did a fabulous job of exposing the students to words like "sarcophagus," not just "mummy," and they created mummified bones out of chicken legs, instead of just reading about Tutankhamen. The lesson ended with an elaborately produced musical of the life and times in Ancient Egypt. This is just the kind of richness and depth that visual-spatial learners need to retain, and later recall, new material.

By traditional standards, sometimes visual-spatial learners may not seem ready to tackle higher level material because they may not have yet mastered the steps that their more sequential counterparts have accomplished. But it is the challenging, meaningful material that engages the right hemisphere and will excite them about learning. It is what will motivate them to succeed.

> The best teaching strategy for me was to give me as much information as fast as possible. The faster the better. Something I found interesting and challenging made the experience even better.

Matt's brain

While my children were homeschooled, they had an opportunity to take some outside classes with other homeschoolers. One of those classes was Spanish. Visual-spatial learners do not typically master foreign languages unless they are involved in a total immersion program, but here my kids were, number one and two in the class. I asked Matt to tell me how he was able to learn Spanish so well (I didn't bother telling him it wasn't supposed to be a strength of his!). He proceeded to draw, in great detail, (rather than try to tell me verbally, of course) just how his brain worked.

Matt's "satellites" (ears) receive the information, which is then forwarded to the "Picture-Making Building" which transforms the signals into pictures. Those pictures then travel to the "Picture Stamping" area, which "puts what the picture means on the picture." Finally, the picture traveled to the "Filing Building" where all images are stored for later recollection. What I particularly enjoyed hearing about was where all the employees (who were responsible for receiving signals, stamping the pictures and filing) live: Employee Paradise, a fenced-in village complete with swimming pool, a small store and a single outhouse! It was amazing to me then, and remains so today, that at age eight, Matt clearly understood that he learned in pictures and that those images would require translation within his brain to be able to communicate verbally. And that was just for the information he knew in English! The foreign words, I would assume, might have required another step altogether.

Matt recently returned to a traditional classroom because homeschooling was not meeting his extreme social needs: He longed for crowds of kids at lunch time, an entire team to play with in P.E. and to participate in drama—all things I was challenged to provide in a school of just two students. Initially, he really struggled to remember to turn in his homework, take his lunch box and/or his backpack and other routine tasks that for him had not been routine for many years. Yet, he was capable of elaborate inventions, detailed drawings and wonderfully creative and funny stories. A friend of mine commented, "So, Matt, do you mean to tell me that you can build this remarkable bowling alley out of gift wrapping tubes and tape (the ball even returned to the bowler), but you can't remember to take your lunchbox to school each morning?" To which Matt replied, "Yup! I'm giftedly visual-spatial!" Lacking in self-esteem Matt isn't, but he certainly understands his own strengths and weaknesses. Chapter 5 will offer insights and specific tips for successfully navigating the challenges topsy-turvy kids face in school, especially getting and staying organized.

Making life, at home and at school, funny, silly, colorful and big is effective for auditory-sequential and visual-spatial learners alike. The success of Bill Nye the Science Guy, with his crazy antics, loud background music and silly characters is proof that real learning can happen in even the silliest of environments. And why shouldn't learning be fun beyond the earliest grades? Acquiring new knowledge should be an adventure for all, a passionate exploration into worlds unknown!

Succeeding as a Visual-Spatial in an Auditory-Sequential Classroom

Yes, it can be done! But not without support and help. Topsy-turvy kids can succeed and thrive in any environment (home, school, and more), if, like any other child, they have the tools and support they need. If you and your children's teachers are open and willing to honor your children's specific learning styles, there is nothing holding your topsy-turvy kids back. It doesn't require dramatic changes on the part of the curriculum, you, the teachers or, best of all, the children. Recognizing strengths and weaknesses, a willingness to work with each other and honoring individual differences are all that's required.

> ...When I discovered ... the writings on Visual-Spatial Learners...it was like the light finally shown! It has put so many of my difficulties in life in perspective. I just never believed I was Ok as I was! Now I do and it is very exciting and is changing my life immensely! I continue to read voraciously about this topic and feel more and more liberated every day!

A good first step in working with your children's teachers is to expose them to ***Upside-Down Brilliance: The Visual-Spatial Learner***, especially Chapter 13, Teaching Techniques that Work. This book is a wonderful resource, particularly for teachers. It contains countless anecdotes of actual students, actual teachers and actual classroom techniques that are effective. Teachers will relate well to Linda Silverman's writing style, experiences and humor, as she, too, was a classroom teacher for many years. She understands the challenges of catering to each unique student and she presents tactics that are simple to implement, yet highly effective for all learners.

Beyond offering this important work to your children's teachers, meet with them early in the school year to discuss your children's needs. Ask if they would be interested in some strategies for reaching your child and other visual-spatial learners in the classroom. If they say yes, present a few key ideas. Give them a chance; the concept of the visual-spatial learner, while relatively new, is spreading. Many teachers have heard the term, some will understand its implications for the student and learning environment, most will not yet realize just how easy it is to incorporate successful accommodations.

> I remember thinking in high school how much nicer it would be if the teacher would just take a minute or two at the beginning of class to briefly state (or better yet show with a flow chart or some other visual aid) the main path and goal of the lecture. Something like, "Today we are going to see how the angles and sides of the triangle are related. It is possible to determine one, given the other, and here's how that works..." It was so much easier to learn things when I had the basic concept on which to hang all the little details in my mind, rather than trying to piece a lot of little details into the big picture, which is how I usually spent the first 15 minutes of a 35 minute lecture where the teacher wouldn't tell me where he/she was going.

Staying focused and on-track

Many topsy-turvy children struggle to stay focused and on-task in their work. The reasons vary for each child but may include and are certainly not limited to:

- Growing bored with the material (particularly if it is being presented in an auditory format only) either because it is too low level or because they cannot create images for the words they are hearing.

- Having so much visual stimulation in the room that it distracts rather than reinforces the new material.

- Central auditory processing issues that are causing background noises such as air conditioning and the jostling of papers to compete with the teacher's voice.

- Undetected vision issues that make it difficult to see the board or the teacher or even to read.

- Possessing a vivid imagination that offers far more appealing distractions and allows them to escape to other worlds of their creation and completely tune out. Often these are the students diagnosed as having AD/HD.

- AD/HD.

When new material is presented following the suggestions in **Upside-Down Brilliance** and within these pages, most students will demonstrate dramatic changes in their ability to focus on learning and retaining new information. (Please see Chapter 3 of **Upside-Down Brilliance** for identifying signs of and specific accommodations for children with central auditory processing disorder; Chapter 11 for information related to AD/HD and Chapter 9 for a discussion of vision issues and therapy.)

I recently met a mother of a topsy-turvy preschooler at a conference in Indianapolis. She had an excellent recommendation for helping her son keep his attention focused on the teacher: she asked permission for him to wear a baseball cap in class and taught him that the bill of the hat, which he could easily see while wearing the hat, must always be pointed toward his teacher. This way, he couldn't find himself visually distracted by watching out the window or staring at pictures. By keeping the bill aimed in the teacher's direction, he was able to stay better focused on what she was saying.

I also found a successful trick in the classroom by letting my topsy-turvy preschoolers have a small, quiet object to manipulate while they were listening. Small beanbags, balloons filled with flour (then tightly secured), hackey sacks and Silly Putty (as long as there's no carpeting to threaten!) are great for this and help the student to focus attention where needed.

For wiggle worms, like mine, I've created a tool that I must admit has only worked with mixed results. I'll tell you in case it works for your child, though. When we homeschooled, Matt had the worst time staying in his seat. He was constantly tipping his chair back on two legs, climbing onto the table, or sitting in all sorts of awkward positions that almost always made him fall out! There were many days I had to take his chair away from him and have him stand at the worktable because I was afraid he was going to hurt himself! Finally, I had my husband cut some simple 1 ½" PVC pipes about six to eight inches long. Each kid got two pipes to place under his feet. They were forced to sit properly in their chairs in order to be able to roll the pipes (gently) with the bottoms of their feet. Now, this only had moderate success because it inevitably led to pipes that got away, then I had missing children grasping for their pipes under the table. (At least the room was carpeted so the pipes couldn't get too far!) But it did seem to help them to stay seated, with six legs on the ground (four from the chair, two from the student!) at all times. I haven't had the courage to ask if Matt is sitting properly or not in his new classroom but I think I'll wait until his teacher brings it up!

> Copying from the board is difficult for C. She says she feels rushed and cannot even think about what books to choose for homework.

This is a problem for many visual-spatial learners. If at all possible, ask your children's teachers if daily and weekly assignments can be copied and distributed ahead of time for them, rather than relying on them to copy the material themselves.

Selective hearing

Topsy-turvy kids seem to have selective hearing. You know, they can't hear when they're playing with LEGOs™ and you've called them to come to dinner, but if you're talking about heading out for ice cream, they're the first ones with their shoes on, right? This may actually be a matter of not being capable of listening to more than one thing at a time, something Linda Silverman refers to as "peripheral audition" (similar to peripheral vision). Or, your children may be so engrossed in the activity they are participating in that they really don't hear you at all. One mother had this advice:

> When my son sinks into a deep focus working on something and cannot "hear" us calling him or talking with him, my mother (his grandmother) discovered that if she just used a regular, pleasant voice and called my son by an unexpected name, my son would break a smile and look up at her correcting her about his name. Usually I use a name of one of his favorite [movie] characters...

I've found that a light touch to the shoulder can stir my kids from their activities, too. Don't expect responses or action if you've issued a request without having their full attention. They very likely have not heard you. If there is music or other noise in the background, turn it down or off. Sometimes just the change in volume will capture their attention.

Reading

> I read by visually assimilating large blocks of text in an instant, translating sometimes 10-20 word chunks into movies and pictures in my head without translating into language (I know that sounds odd but that's the best way I can explain it). I can read surprisingly fast, but when I read aloud I often unconsciously transpose words or reword sentences. Strangely, I can make myself read the words in a linear mode (both silently and aloud), but have a lot of trouble assimilating their contextual meaning that way.

Like most children, visual-spatial learners have a burning desire to learn to read. They recognize early on that the answers to their questions lie in books. They want to learn all there is to know of a specific passion and then they want to move on. However, learning to read can be an added challenge to the child who thinks in pictures, rather than in words, and to the student who learns whole-to-part, not step-by-step.

> Learning to read was the single largest problem I faced as a child. Until the age of 14 I did not read anything that was not required for a class assignment. I would do anything and everything I could think of to get out of reading. This went on until I discovered something I WANTED to read, then you could not get me away from books.

This is true for many VSLs. They become so intensely interested in a subject that they will read everything they can get their hands on about it, even if they decode slowly and reading is challenging for them.

Most children today are taught to read phonetically: a sequential process where learning the sounds of letters leads to learning the sounds of blends, then combining those to learn whole words. Gradually the learning moves from words to sentences to paragraphs. The process is slow and not meaningful to topsy-turvy kids. Most VSLs learn to read best by using a process of recognizing and comparing whole words, not letter sounds and blends. The visual-spatial student is capable of filing and storing countless images that can be easily retrieved, images of words and how they sound.

> If you were looking at the Mona Lisa, would you just look left to right, line by line? A paragraph is no different than a painting— why would you want to look at it only one way?

Visual-spatial children should be taught to read sight words, particularly words that have been decorated with color and characters. Students should select words they are curious or passionate about first to build a picture vocabulary in their minds. These might be words of animals (monkey, horse, alligator) or places they've visited (Disneyland, beach, lake), of people in their lives (teacher, aunt, cousin) or occupations in the community (doctor, fireman, teacher), etc. Help them create a colorful collection of their sight words in an album or special box. When Sam was in preschool, he had a key ring with each word on brightly colored paper. He loved reviewing his collection of sight words and adding to it. Eventually he could combine sight words into stories, adding to the fun. Look through magazines with your children to find more interesting words they want to be able to read and add to their collection. Encourage your children to use magnetic letters on the refrigerator to spell and respell their words throughout the day.

Keep in mind the use of humor to help the new knowledge become permanent and use the child's collection of sight words to create silly sentences and stories. This will likely introduce adjectives into the collection, which makes the game even more fun! Tongue twisters and rhyming words make reading games lively and challenge them to create new images for similar looking words or words that have similar blends. As visual-spatial learners, these children excel at seeing patterns. Create books of words that rhyme so that they can readily "see" that some words have the same sounds and blends as words they already know. You can create really funny books when your children are ready to learn homonyms (one of my kids was really stuck on a "bare bear" at one time!).

> I have a photographic memory, but my biggest challenge is to have the patience to sit down and read things in order to have it impressed in my memory. Often, I would take tests and be able to close my eyes and reread the page from where the answer existed.

Topsy-turvy kids can also be taught to speed read. This meets several of their needs. First, most visual-spatial kids do not read every single word anyway so teaching them to skip over certain unimportant words (articles, excessive adjectives, and the like) helps them to cut to the chase. These kids prefer to get the big picture and get to it quickly. Verbose they are not, and they won't tolerate reading unnecessary verbiage, either. Second, many topsy-turvy kids are at least mildly deficient in attention span. Speed reading helps keep them on track and focused on the material. It is not a laid back activity to scan through a page and be able to recall key facts. Last, successful speed reading will serve to create lasting images that can be easily recalled: the jist of the material or story will be what is read and remembered. Initially, students of speed reading may need to scan a page a few times but this technique is often more effective than slow reading it just once. Allow your children to use colored highlighters to note key points (make photocopies if you don't want the book marked up) that they may also want to detail in their notes or drawings later, depending on the material.

> A lot of documentation can be read in a Z like pattern. The first and last sentences hold the key information, and the middle part helps flesh out the picture. I read the first sentence or so in a left to right fashion, then I grab the middle part as my eyes move back from right to left, then read the last bit left to right.
>
> Other types of writing have different shapes. Newspaper articles are upside down pyramids, with the most important information at the top.
>
> Opinion pieces are sometimes regular pyramids, with the conclusion at the end. For these, I sometimes start at the end first.
>
> The Z and pyramids are the most common, but occasionally things are written in spirals. In those cases, the key information is in the middle.
>
> Sometimes I may scan a paragraph more than once in more than one way. If I'm having trouble understanding it, I'll sometimes even read it backwards. That can make key words and phrases "pop out."
>
> And sometimes I just read "normally," one line at a time, left to right. But it's still a picture. If it's difficult, I'll ingest one sentence at a time. For normal reading, I read a paragraph at a time.

When I was a preschool teacher I saw many instances where children resisted learning to read because they felt that their parents would stop reading to them. The bonds formed during such close times as when a parent is reading to a child are very special and not something most children want to relinquish. Reassure your children that you will continue to read to them, even after they have mastered reading. Though my boys are 9 and 11 today, some of our most treasured times together are when we're cuddled up on my bed sharing a good story. Because visual-spatial kids can create such elaborate pictures in their imaginations to go with the story you are reading them, remember to include books of fantasy and those with strong visual imagery.

For more information on teaching topsy-turvy kids to read, see Betty Maxwell's ideas in "Wholes and Patterns: Reading Help for Struggling Gifted Visual-Spatial Learners" in the Spring 2003 *Gifted Education Communicator*.

Spelling

> His spelling is terrible in writing assignments, although he actually does quite well on spelling tests, where he claims he forms a mental picture of the word.

Spelling seems to be universally challenging for visual-spatial children and adults. I do hope this website visitor, a VSL adult, will forgive me for using this particular anecdote, but it is so telling of the difficulty these learners have with spelling.

> The low grades were *do* to the fact that I was *so board* with the classes I felt it was a *waist* of my time to even do the work. (Emphasis added)

Thank goodness spell checkers were invented. For those who think in images, not words, it can be very difficult to create pictures that incorporate letters, particularly pictures that will live on as memorable images in the visual learner's mind. Color is a great tool for accomplishing this. Taking the "EI" in WEIGHT and making them a different color, even larger type, helps to secure the rule, or for them the image, that the E precedes the I. This is an effective trick for nearly all spelling words, particularly those with unusual or rule-breaking spelling. My sons had a teacher who taught her students to actually place "rule-breaking" spelling words in jail, behind bars. The image of the word having been imprisoned for breaking the rules would stick in their memory. Here's one Matt did for the word, "reign" because the "g" is a rule breaker, serving little purpose in the spelling of the word:

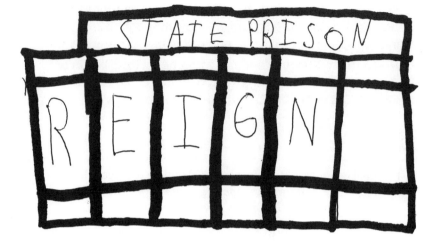

However, if color or jail bars don't secure the image, try adding characters around the letters and creating a whole story around the word itself. Remember, humor will engage the right hemisphere; color and size will help it to be retained.

For example, consider the word, "MOUNTAIN." There are several opportunities for creating actual mountains out of the letters M, N and A. Using a full piece of paper, write the spelling word using pictures of what the word represents. Perhaps our "MOUNTAIN" has climbers on the O or the I. A whole story can be created about the climbers ascending certain letters.

Use any trick that will help the spelling of this word to stay in the child's visual memory. Enlist your children's help in creating ridiculous stories and drawings. This will make the images easier for them to remember. Don't place any boundaries on what their stories include. They need to create the tales, store them and be able to recall them, so let them use what works for them. Sam made up this silly story to remember how to spell, "friend" correctly:

FRIEND

"These **FRI**es from **FRI**day's sure taste good at the day's end!"

"You're right, **FRI**end!"

If your visual-spatial children have successfully created an image of the word in their minds, they will be able to spell that word forward and backward. To test whether the image your children have created has a permanent, retrievable place in their memory or "file cabinet," as Matt would say, ask your children to spell the word in reverse. If they can't do it, they need to work on some other technique such as color, humor, size, etc. to secure their image of the word until they are able to spell it correctly forward and backward.

Writing

For many VSLs, the physical act of handwriting is slow to develop. Writing has got to be one of the most sequential tasks we ask of our topsy-turvy kids. Even the direction of the letters is confusing. To a visual-spatial learner who can easily rotate and manipulate images mentally, the letters d, b, p and q are identical shapes! The only exception I can think of is writing in Japanese, using beautiful artistic characters to represent words and sentences. I wonder if Japanese visual-spatial children struggle to write traditional Japanese or if they are able to find joy in the art form that they create? But in English, to learn the direction of each letter, then link those letters into words, words into sentences, sentences into paragraphs, paragraphs into stories or reports or essays—yikes!

Most of us are right-handed, the hand controlled by the left hemisphere. But for topsy-turvy kids this is the weaker hemisphere and the least relied upon. Relying on their left hemisphere can be exhausting work, physically and mentally. In the early school years, while your topsy-turvy children are learning to write their first letters and words, offer them plenty of breaks and protein-filled snacks as they practice. Helpful tools include sponge grips or grips with finger indentations, so they hold their writing utensils properly. Also, watch for hands that are gripping too tightly or writing with more pressure than needed, which will tire your children more quickly. Words of praise and encouragement go far, particularly for the child struggling to accomplish what may be coming much easier to his auditory-sequential peers.

Is keyboarding a more valuable skill than handwriting?

If your children struggle to complete assignments because their fine motor coordination is poor, try teaching them keyboarding skills and allowing them to type their papers. Many topsy-turvy kids are quite proficient on the computer and at an early age, so enjoy teaching them how to increase their speed by developing their keyboarding skills.

> G was three the first time we let him use the laptop as a word processor. He was very much enjoying typing the alphabet forward, backwards, using TAB and getting it evenly spaced. He seemed distracted, and kept looking down the hall. He finally ran to his blocks and made an alphabet in the keyboard configuration, QWERT, etc.

One of the first things my children began to learn once they were out of traditional school and in homeschool was keyboarding. My husband and I recognized many years ago that while he was in Woodshop and I was in Typing, I was the one learning the most valuable skill in today's computer-literate world. Few boys were in that Typing 101 class of mine and I wonder today how many type like my husband, hunt-and-peck style, with only their index fingers and thumbs! If we could look into the future, we would no doubt see that the skills of handwriting had become obsolete but the skills of typing would continue to be prized.

There are a number of keyboarding programs available for young kids. In fact, I've even seen modified keyboards designed for smaller fingers and hands! These children will be using computers all of their lives, why not teach them early on and let them use this technology to their advantage when they need it most? It may very well put an end to the battles over handwriting, help to speed the process of completing homework assignments and getting their thoughts on paper. In the not-so-distant future, the art of handwriting will be just that, an art. Already we can bypass any necessary writing by using computers. Even signing checks is becoming obsolete with the availability of paying bills online. So, end the fighting over perfect penmanship and allow keyboarding to become a priority in your children's acquisition of skills.

The organization of writing

Organizing one's writing is another challenge for visual-spatial learners. The entire structure of an outline is based on sequential thinking. Luckily, there are products on the market today, like Inspiration® and Kidspiration®, which can turn a student's image of a report or story, actually "web" versions of them, into sequentially written documents. These products work the same way a topsy-turvy kid's mind does: by starting with the whole, big picture, then breaking it down into the details.

One adult VSL has this advice:

I realize that because I'm a vsl I think wholistically, all concepts considered simultaneously. I started doing brain dumps while writing, letting ideas flow out all at once. Everything comes out fast and jumbled but then it's easy to organize and reword. It's much more efficient for me to write this way than to sit and sit while I think of the perfectly worded next sentence.

Another approach to creating outlines for reports and other written works is to let the student write the entire report first and build the outline from the finished piece. This is sometimes not how the teacher would prefer to see the product created, but it follows a comfortable learning pattern for visual-spatial learners: starting with the big picture, then working toward the smaller details.

Math facts

> I remember being in 3rd grade and having a terrible time learning my multiplication tables ... by the time I was in junior high, I had developed my own solution for this. I found that if I wrote down whatever it was that I needed to memorize on a piece of blank, unlined, white paper—I could visually see it when I was taking a test. Just as if I had the paper right in front of me. I actually had one teacher that thought that I was praying during her tests, because the images were clearer to me with my eyes closed.

Rote memorization of math facts can be drudgery for any child, but particularly so for the visual-spatial learner. Perhaps because, as whole-to-part thinkers, they are being presented with the facts and details first and would prefer instead to just get to the bigger picture, then master the details? I know that both of my children excelled in advanced math concepts such as algebra and geometry, before mastering their times tables. Not many teachers would let that kind of acceleration happen without a good foundation of basic math, but I knew my kids were hungry for bigger picture material and real world applications. Perhaps topsy-turvy kids struggle with rote memorization because it is challenging to create a lasting, permanent image for numbers, especially numbers added, multiplied, subtracted or divided? Whatever the reason, memorizing math facts seems to top the charts in homework battles. One mother wrote me:

> She does seem to be more of a concept versus a detail person—she could solve simple math word problems (you've gone once around the room, and you're going to go three in total. How many do you have left?) well before she could count (still doesn't very well) but she totally understands the concept of numbers and how they work.

Dr. Lynn Hellerstein, a behavioral optometrist my children visit, advises parents teaching math facts to their visual-spatial children to hold flashcards in a position that forces the student to look to the upper left to see the card, under the premise that, for the learner who relies more on the right hemisphere, this will help secure the image of that math fact.

Visual-spatial learners can learn their multiplication facts in just two weeks if they are shown the whole number system, then walked through the parts and helped to create images of the facts they do not already know. When I have tried this, the kids I've worked with were surprised at how many facts they already knew when we started. The grid can be intimidating initially and children immediately feel they will not be able to conquer it.

x	0	1	2	3	4	5	6	7	8	9	10
0											
1											
2											
3											
4											
5											
6											
7											
8											
9											
10											

Here's how to walk your child through the grid:

First, you can demonstrate that the two rows of zeros are easily eliminated, since anything times 0 equals 0. Next, you show that the rows of 1's are simple, since anything times 1 equals itself. Most children agree that the 10's are easy because you just put a zero after the multiplier. At this point, demonstrate that the child only has to learn half of the total chart because one half is a mirror image of the other. You can show this visually by folding the grid on the diagonal.

You've just taught the commutative principle: $a \times b = b \times a$. Every child I've shown this to begins to feel relief at this point!

The next step is to ask if the child can count by two, which most have learned already. If she can count by two, she can multiply by two so you move on to the 5's, which most visual-spatial children find are even easier than the 2's because they can see the pattern of the answer ending in 0 or 5. And, like the 2's, she can skip count on her fingers, counting by 5's until she's reached the multiple she was seeking.

Next come the 3's. Schoolhouse Rock has a great video called "Multiplication Rock" that uses songs to count by various numbers. I remember these as commercials on ABC® television during Saturday morning cartoons and many of the songs have stuck with me to this day. (The commercials are even available on DVD. You can learn math facts, American History, grammar rules, and more.) For some reason, the song they created for the 3's is particularly memorable and I've seen it help many kids learn to multiply by 3's success-fully.

Stop and show your child just how many rows of the grid she's covered already! Remember, huge doses of praise will help the motivation to continue.

Now it's time to tackle the 9's. There are many tricks for 9's including subtracting one from the number of nines being multiplied, then find a number, which, when added to the first number, results in the sum of nine and you have your answer. For example, in 8×9, you would subtract 1 from 8 leaving 7. What plus 7 equals 9? (2). The answer is 72; since 7 is one less than 8 and 7 plus 2 add up to 9. Also, all the answers to multiples of 9 are mirror images: 18-81, 27-72, 36-63, and 45-54 creating a pattern that many VSLs can remember. You can also show that in a table of all the multiples of 9, while the digit in the tens column increases by one, the digit in the ones column decreases by one:

09

18

27

36

45

54

63

72

81

90

At this point, the original grid of 121 facts has been reduced to just 16! They are: 4 x 4, 4 x 6, 4 x 7, 4 x 8, 6 x 6, 6 x 7, 6 x 8, 7 x 7, 7 x 8, and 8 x 8. Start next with the doubles: 4 x 4, 6 x 6, etc. Doubles seem to be easier than some of the others because they have a natural rhythm. Rhythm stimulates the right hemisphere so rhythmic patterns should always be emphasized. The facts 6 x 6 = 36 and 5 x 5 = 25 are easily remembered because they rhyme.

Fours can be taught as doubling the 2's facts and 6's are just a doubling of the 3's. You can also use clever phrases to secure these facts, such as: When you are 16 you can drive a 4 x 4 (4 x 4 = 16). And 7 x 8 = 56 can be remembered as 5, 6, 7, 8 (56 = 7 x 8). These tricks reduce the number of difficult math facts to only a few—usually six or less. With only 12 empty spots on the grid, remind the child that this equals just six facts they must memorize. Ask her to draw a picture of her favorite things, one picture for each problem. For example, if her favorite animal is a unicorn, she might draw six unicorns each prancing among four flowers. Somewhere in the drawing, she should include "6 x 4 = 24" and "4 x 6 = 24." Ask her to look at her drawing and memorize the details before she goes to bed. If she creates a story to go with the drawing, one that incorporates the math fact, that will help, too. With only six remaining math facts, your child only needs to do one drawing a night for six nights.

After the sixth night of drawings is complete, your child will have mastered the multiplication grid. What a great accomplishment!

Division can be quite difficult for visual-spatial learners, since it is usually in a step-by-step fashion, and these are not step-by-step learners. I have found, however, that if the image of the multiplication fact is truly secure in their mind's eye, my sons can see it in reverse. In other words, if you have to be 16 to drive a 4 x 4 (16 = 4 x 4), they are able to see that 16 divided by 4 equals 4.

Because many visual-spatial learners can create their own methods for long division, do not insist that they show their work. Allow them to devise their own strategy to arrive at an answer and give them additional problems to see if their system works. Gradually increase the difficulty of the problems to test their system. If their teachers insist on seeing the steps they've taken to get to a final solution, teach your children to work in reverse. In other words, they can use their methods (so long as they produce accurate results) to arrive at an answer, and then work backward through the problem to show the steps, or their "work." Even though that's not how they arrived at their answer, it will satisfy the teacher's requirement to show steps toward a solution.

Homework

It can really feel like torture if you and your visual-spatial child are arguing daily to complete homework assignments. Matt, my youngest, could easily think of thousands of things he'd rather do (LEGOs™, K'Nex™, draw, build anything out of tape and toilet paper rolls, etc.), than return to studying his books. The last thing my husband and I are up for is a fight over his homework. I went from being with my child 24 hours a day for the five years we homeschooled to a brief "hello" in the morning and a reunion after 4:00pm. The last thing I had the time or inclination to do with him was argue over completing his schoolwork. With today's busy schedules, for parents and kids alike, I can't imagine that anyone actually has time for such confrontations. Besides, it can't be good for any relationship to know that once reunited at the end of a tiring day, there are going to be blood pressure-rising battles waiting on the home front. Coming home from school is supposed to be a warm cookies and milk event, not a showdown from the Wild West!

So, what's the solution? I'm still working on it, but it includes my son's involvement in creating a balance between getting enough playtime with friends and toys, and getting his work done. The answer includes taking breaks, eating protein snacks, prioritizing, carefully scheduling his afternoons and evenings and maintaining harmony in the home. It includes everyone's understanding of the value of what must be done vs. the value of what they'd prefer to get done. When Matt was homeschooled, there was plenty of time to balance play and work. A classroom of two meant adequate individual attention coupled with few administrative distractions (roll call, handing out papers, collecting papers, lining up, etc.) so that the day's work was completed soon after lunch. But, a return to school to meet his social needs has meant a readjustment of the day for him. (An extensive commute hasn't helped the equation, but we're working on that part, too!)

Reward systems can be an effective tool for motivating reluctant children and ensuring homework is completed. In our family, Movie Night is currently the big reward. The better the week went (in terms of completing homework assignments and chores, general getting along, etc.), the more movie snacks available and the later the bedtime gets extended. I've heard one son say to the other, "Just get your homework done so we can have Movie Night on Friday!" Game Night motivates them, too!

We keep a treasure chest full of inexpensive, though highly desirable, toys and treats like small LEGO™ sets, cars, balsa wood gliding planes, packs of chewing gum, and more. If my children show initiative toward completing their work, do a particularly nice job on an assignment or chore, or I see that they've concentrated hard toward resolving an issue without parental involvement, I'll let them visit the treasure box and select a reward for themselves. If reading is the current Issue of the Month, each child can receive a visit to the treasure chest for completing a book. If cleaning out the cat box has been the Gripe of the Week, same reward. The rewards don't have to be costly or big to work, just something your children would want but can't have without earning.

Sometimes the conflict over homework can really be more about having a say in when it gets done. Resistance sets in if my child comes home from school and is immediately nagged about getting homework started right away. Each day should have an agreed upon starting time for homework. Children must be reminded of other afterschool commitments, then asked to come to an agreement on what time their schoolwork will be completed. Often, just having a say will help encourage the action. (By the way, I've found this tip to be helpful for chores, as well.)

Beyond the elementary years

Help your topsy-turvy children understand the extent and limits of their own strengths and weaknesses, especially as related to their learning styles. When children at any age can look at new material and create for themselves a more effective way to retain that information, they find success throughout their academic careers. Positive learning experiences in the early grades will afford your children the confidence to tackle virtually any subject in later years. They will be able to utilize many of those same techniques for retaining new information in a way that is meaningful and lasting for them.

As your children progress through grade levels, introduce them to timelines, presenting information in graphs, webbing, creating detailed maps and other visual tricks that help information to be retained.

> We discovered fairly early on that we could teach nearly anything if a map was involved.

In upper grades, it is often possible to get an overview of an upcoming lecture from the instructor. This will help your children to grasp the big picture first so that they may understand the parts during the actual talk.

Timed tests are torture for the visual-spatial learner and very tough to avoid in school. Remember the analogy of the computer downloading graphics being equal to the effort it takes these kids to translate their pictures into words? The pressure of timed tests only serves to magnify their anxiety, rendering them helpless and unable to answer the questions at all. Advocacy for your children will no doubt include discussions with their teachers of how to minimize, if not eliminate, timed tests from their program. If, however, this is not possible, and your child will be facing timed tests, you must practice at home. The comfort and safety of home coupled with knowing it is just a practice drill may help to ease the tension when they face the real test in the classroom.

Also, playing games that require them to think fast on their feet, translating images into words quickly may help. These would include Pictionary, Boggle, Trivial Pursuit, Cranium, or any other games with hourglasses where coming up with quick answers is crucial. Try adding an hourglass to Scrabble to encourage faster spelling or to a game of charades to help increase speed in their translation time. Make up your own games with your children's homework material using historical dates, names and places or math facts as the answers. Any practice you can offer, while under time limitations, will help them prepare for classroom-timed tests.

Organizational skills

It is important to note that while the topsy-turvy child or adult may seem hopelessly unorganized, it has been my experience that such a person can truly find a needle in a haystack. Matt, for example, whose room on any given day may look as though multiple tornadoes have hit, never ceases to amaze me in his ability to locate just the perfect LEGO™ piece he was searching for. (The missing homework, on the other hand, you might never find!)

SEQUENTIAL   SPATIAL

Organization will no doubt remain a stumbling block even as your children mature. Be sure to visit office supply stores and other places that carry a variety of products designed to help with organization. Color-coded envelopes, files and pocket folders are perfect for storing specific papers. Colored index cards are a great tool for note taking, and the use of a DayTimer® or Palm Pilot™ to record due dates and appointments are all tools available for the visual-spatial learner. Do you ever wonder why so many organizational products have come on the market in recent years? These must be the inventions of the visual-spatials among us to help themselves and others like them!

Linda Leviton, a member of the Visual-Spatial Resource Access team and a visual-spatial learner herself, writes:

> VSLs are either horizontal or vertical organizers...if they are horizontal, they need a long table (preferably not deep) to put out (and leave out) works in process. If they are vertical, they need places to create stacks. I bought myself one of those paper sorters with cubbies and have it right next to my computer (with labels for each section) and that's how I do it. (L. Leviton, personal communication, May 31, 2004)

While your children select their own personal methods of organization, make sure they are selecting techniques and products for themselves. This is not an area that lends itself to any outside input! The choices they make must have meaning for them and no one else, so try to keep your ideas out of the mix. One former topsy-turvy kid, now a topsy-turvy adult, wrote this interesting suggestion for helping with organization skills:

> I used to be THE most disorganized person, but today, I am pretty darn good at it. A few years ago, my sister gave me a Game boy with Tetris, and I swear, that has helped me in this area. When I first started playing Tetris, my high scores barely reached 500, and now they're one million plus! At work, I'm the one who organizes everything, and it always makes me laugh out loud when people say I'm organized, but I never, ever was until recently!

When we homeschooled, each of my children used a Teacher's Planner to record their daily assignments in. There are several varieties available including ones that show a week-at-a-glance or a month-at-a-glance. You can find them at local teacher's supply stores. We used these as checklists, too, which added to their sense of accomplishment to see each assignment crossed off. Then, the completed week was added to a log to record the entire school year's work.

Linda Leviton also advised:

> As for schoolwork, I have one word for you...pockets. Forget binders and putting holes in things. They need something they can shove papers into, and if you color code the pockets you have a better chance of the right paper getting into the right pocket. My preference is a folder with each class having it's own colored pockets (one in front and one on back)...front is for current work or something to be turned in, back is for reference or past work. Just don't expect them to punch holes or get papers in sections that involve opening or closing anything; stuffing is what they do best.
> (L. Leviton, personal communication, May 31, 2004)

Matt's personal method for ensuring that he remembers to take his homework folder, lunchbox and water bottle to school every day is to pile them all up at his place on the kitchen table. Then, when he finishes breakfast, he takes it all immediately to the car. The few times he has left one of those items somewhere other than the kitchen table, they didn't make it to school. The consequence for not remembering one's lunchbox is pretty tough to handle but I think it's important for natural consequences to occur in order for my children to become self-sufficient.

Try to maintain a consistent family schedule from week to week. This would include eating dinner together at the same time every night as well as setting aside the same time every afternoon or evening for play, homework and daily chores. A large calendar for recording each family member's schedule is helpful, too. Use it to show everyone's commitments from sports practices to work schedules, field trip days to long-term assignments, holidays and other days off. I've found that encouraging my kids to record the due dates for assignments three to four days prior to the actual due date has really helped avoid last minute all-nighters. The extra built-in time allows room for editing, project revisions, etc. and a more relaxed approach to the deadline. Having a master calendar also allows visual-spatial learners (notoriously known for lacking a sense of time) to see how long until Christmas, the last day of school, their birthday or other events they are anticipating.

Consider creating a specific time for computer and television use. If this is built into the daily schedule, it's easier to understand why mom is enforcing the homework hour at that time, not allowing procrastination, or distraction of the TV or computer, to fester into another argument. We use a timer in our house to eliminate conflicts about what time the computer game or TV show started. The timer is not arbitrary. It rings, turn over.

"A place for everything and everything in its place"—not an easy trick for topsy-turvy kids, but a technique that will last them a lifetime. I seldom lose my car keys because they go in the exact same place every time I return home. We have a small bookshelf set aside just for library books so when the due date comes, we're not scrambling to find them. I do believe it's important for kids to have their rooms kept the way they would like them, but they must be able to locate their clothing, sports equipment and other items in a reasonable amount of time. We also insist that there be a clear path from the door to the bedside in case we have to go to them in the night—there have been too many episodes of bare feet on toys to count! Inexpensive containers, even shoeboxes and plastic food tubs, make great sorting accessories for small toys. We maintain an entire closet exclusively for construction toys.

Advanced preparation is critical. Pack backpacks and lunchboxes the night before. Sometimes, we even load the car up the night before to try and eliminate morning hassles. Have clothing for the next day already selected, Matt lays his out on the end of his bed each night. Where we live the weather changes frequently and without notice so we keep the car prepared with extra light jackets, sometimes a complete change of clothing and, *always*, snacks. (Part of this over preparedness is that Matt's commute to school is 52 miles, one-way.)

In Appendix C, you will find a Survival Checklist for parents, that summarizes many of the points in this chapter.

Understanding Your Options

Auditory-sequential learners must have created modern-day schools. Most teachers and most curricula are sequential. Typically, a student learns A, followed by B, followed by C, to arrive at Answer D. It's a tried and true pattern that has been perpetuated for generations. Generations of auditory-sequential learners, that is. But what if your child is the kind of student who had already accurately arrived at Answer D, and had no need for Steps A, B or C in order to get there? What if your child's "D" was the same as the instructor's, but she was marked down because she could not show her work, could not offer Steps A, B, or C to explain, in a sequential fashion, how Answer D came to be?

What if your child was not able to concentrate on the minute details of any given subject? What if your child has to know where the lesson is headed, the big picture of the entire discussion? Without that understanding, the dates, names and places are meaningless bits of information lost in a sea of irretrievable data with no connection to any significant knowledge. What if, even though your child understands the events that led to a particular war, the key players involved, etc., she can't recite the exact date of a specific battle and her grade then suffers? Anyone can see that she's intelligent, but she still feels like a failure, academically. Such is the plight of the visual-spatial learner. These topsy-turvy kids are often bright students by any measure, except by traditional school standards.

Schools have alternated in their assessment of her intellect and capability. Teachers with a sense of humor and irony (usually math and English—subjects where an occasional flash of insight on the student's part is a huge help), think she's very bright and consistently recommend her for more challenging work. Getting strokes from a couple of teachers each year has given her confidence—she knows she "belongs" with the smart kids and is not herself a dummy or a slacker.

History and science teachers—classes where mastery of thousands of unrelated details is important—see her as unexceptional. This causes a problem as she gets closer to graduation. Since the headmaster is a history teacher, he sees K as just another ordinary student. He will not be providing a glowing letter of recommendation for her college applications.

She always gets the "impossible" extra credit question right—but gets brainlock on multiple-choice questions. Her scores on standardized tests are average and get worse if there's a lot of time pressure.

Another critical fact about visual-spatial learners is that what might appear as "daydreaming" can be serious learning. Steve Haas wrote in "Classroom Identification of Visual-Spatial Learners":

Then there is the student whose notebook is blank, and so is his face, as he gazes, usually up and to the side, out the nearest window. "Billy! Pay attention and start taking notes!" may be just the right tweak to get the daydreamer back on task. But for the VSL, gazing up and to the side is where he stores and can access complicated conceptual material in mental visual file folders. While he appears to be daydreaming, he may actually be actively inputting and processing the lesson. By jolting him out of his trance, you may have just burst his concentration bubble. (p. 19).

Topsy-turvy kids may, in fact, be deeply involved in the act of creating and filing their mental images of new material when it appears they are intently gazing out the window or tuning out. To interrupt that moment, especially by assuming that they are daydreaming, would be to cause them to lose that image and, then, that new information. Even at a young age, your visual-spatial learners are taking in information from all around and processing it the only way they know how. They may be unable to explain what they are learning until the picture has fully formed in their minds. I received this from an astute mother:

Don't assume your VSL isn't watching and absorbing information. G revealed to us all at once (2 ½ years old) that he could identify the entire alphabet (upper and lower case) pretty much self-taught through videos, puzzles and my singing of songs. He didn't learn the alphabet song until two years later. He consistently surprises us as having been listening, watching, absorbing the whole time about many things.

Non-traditional schooling

Non-traditional schooling (which includes a wide variety of options in lieu of, or in combination with, traditional schooling) is much easier for today's families to incorporate into their lifestyles than ever before due to the advent of the Internet and widespread availability of virtual classrooms and online courses. The very nature of a non-traditional learning environment dictates that it will be created to meet the specific needs of your child. Here are some options:

Homeschooling

Some trees grow very tall and straight and large in the forest, close to each other. But some must stand by themselves or they won't grow at all. (Oliver Wendell Holmes)

The story goes that Thomas Edison was expelled from public school before the third grade, sent home to his mother with a note that he was "addle-brained." His mother, knowing her son to be anything but addled, made the decision to homeschool young Thomas and the rest is history.

Edison is far from the only distinguished person in history to have been successfully homeschooled. Other famous home-schoolers include: Albert Einstein, Leonardo da Vinci, George and Martha Washington, Abraham Lincoln, Winston Churchill, Mark Twain, Sally Ride, Franklin Roosevelt, Abigail Adams, Alexander Graham Bell, Florence Nightingale, Hans Christian Anderson, Agatha Christie, C.S. Lewis, General MacArthur, Clara Barton and many, many more!

Homeschooling is currently legal in all 50 states. While restrictions and testing vary greatly from state to state. Visit the National Home Educator's Network at www.nhen.com for details in your state. American families are free to educate their children at home. For students who march to the beat of a different drummer, this can mean freedom from traditional

schedules and the time to study when their body is best
suited for it. It means incorporating modified curricula to
meet each child's unique needs. Homeschooling eliminates
timed tests (an area in which visual-spatial learners face a
serious handicap because of the time it takes to translate
their images into words and numbers), perfect penmanship
and other limitations that can destroy the topsy-turvy child's
self-esteem. It also affords the time and freedom to pursue
passions and an escape from the pressures to conform to a
way of thinking and learning that are completely foreign to
VSLs. It can mean the difference between academic failure
and enthusiastic performance, from negative self-esteem to
positive, and from despising learning in general to becoming
passionate about the acquisition of new knowledge. If your
children are asking to be homeschooled, take their concerns
seriously. Investigate if leaving their current school is an
option for your family. Homeschooling doesn't have to be
costly and I've known a number of dual-income families who
make it work.

When I made the decision to homeschool, I was initially
overwhelmed and greatly intimidated. What if I didn't
remember 5th grade math? What were all those grammar rules
I had supposedly memorized but now forgotten? I had no idea
who conquered whom nor when. (And why is history all about
who conquered whom and when, anyway?) When they
announced they wanted to learn Latin, I panicked. I'd never
had Latin. How was I going to teach them something I had
never been exposed to? But, I quickly learned something that
became one of the greatest lessons I've ever taught my kids:
I didn't have to know everything. I found that I could learn
the material right alongside them. Just because I was officially
their teacher, that didn't mean I had to be the Keeper of All
Knowledge. In learning Latin with them (and many other
subjects since), I was able to teach them that you are never
too old to learn and that learning can be fun and exciting at
any age. I never wanted our learning at home to be about my
pouring information into their heads, but rather, about the
discovery–together–of new ideas, historical facts, and, yes,
grammatical rules.

> Education is not the filling of a pail, but the lighting of a fire.
> (William Butler Yeats)

If you're interested in pursuing homeschooling, I've included some resources in Appendix B.

Homeschooling, admittedly, is not for everyone. It can involve dramatic changes in family structure, particularly if both parents are working outside the home. It can put enormous strain, financially and emotionally, on the parent primarily responsible for the children's education. When I counsel families who are thinking of homeschooling, I often advise that the parent who takes on the responsibility for schooling their children must have a reliable and strong support system. This usually involves a spouse, or nearby family member, who can back you up. Someone to say, "Tag! You're it!" when they need a break, someone to help enforce the rules, someone to act as "principal." It can be very challenging and draining to be all things to your children. As a homeschool parent you are the teacher of multiple subjects at many levels, as well as principal, nurse, janitor, curriculum coordinator, chef, and, oh yeah, parent, all in one, all of the time.

It can also be demanding to have to answer to family and friends why your family has chosen this path, why traditional schooling—something that works for the vast majority and, as some believe, is the basis for our democracy—isn't good enough for you. Do I sound like I've been through this? We spent nearly five wonderful years homeschooling and I wouldn't have changed a thing. It allowed my children's self-esteem to blossom, their skills to flourish and gave them the basis to honor and value their own strengths as well as understand their limitations and weaknesses. I learned more in studying with them than I ever did in my own grade school years and the time spent together and memories created can never be taken from us or rivaled.

One of the greatest benefits to homeschooling, besides having the luxury of creating customized curricula for each child, was that it becomes a way of life. With no one else's schedule to adhere to, we were able to truly enjoy each day: waking when we were rested, eating when we were hungry, studying a subject for as long as we wanted. My children found great pleasure in being able to "immerse" in a subject and not be rushed off to another activity by a loud school bell. Also, because time-consuming administrative duties like handing out and collecting papers, taking roll and lining up are eliminated, a full school day is much shorter (Colorado law states a full day is just four hours), leaving time to pursue hobbies, music, sports and other outside interests.

Homeschooling, like other alternative educational options, can be done on a trial period if you are uncertain it will work for you and your children. Consider spending a few weeks during the summer, or perhaps taking a full semester, to see if it feels like an option that will suit your family. You can always go back to regular school if it doesn't work. You can also attempt a partial homeschooling situation, or combination of traditional schooling (say, during the morning hours) with homeschooling (in the afternoon). Many school districts allow homeschoolers to participate in music and sports activities even though they are not enrolled as full-day students.

Homeschooling doesn't mean you have to be the only instructor. I've known families who've hired tutors for specific subjects (hiring a college student for foreign language or math, for example) and many businesses offer daytime classes for homeschoolers. In our hometown, we found an art studio and a Tae Kwon Do school that did this. We also used distance learning courses to supplement Sam's curriculum for a couple of years. There are a number of correspondence and on-line courses available on the Internet (see Appendix B for more information on this). Also, there are a great many on-line support lists offering tips and resources for home-schooling families. You will also likely find local support groups that focus on sharing resources, offering socialization opportunities for your children, even groups that provide cooperative learning situations.

If you find that homeschooling works as an option for your children, never threaten to send them back to traditional school as punishment. They need to know that the schooling environment you create together is a safe place where they can be nurtured and educated for as long as needed. Listen carefully and respond to your children's needs. If they ask to return to school, consider what it is they are missing and what the trade-offs are in returning.

Unschooling

Unschooling is the practice of allowing children to follow, exclusively, their passions and pursuits believing that the skills of reading and mathematics are a natural by-product of pursuing one's interests. I've known a number of families who have had great success with this method of education. Granted, their children were not necessarily reading at age six, as most traditionally schooled students are, but they did learn to read. Unschooling is about honoring the child's time-frame for achieving certain milestones, especially reading, writing and arithmetic. When the student expresses an interest in mathematics, then math is taught. When the child starts asking questions about history, then that subject is pursued. Education is all on the student's timetable and at their interest level.

We tried unschooling ...for about a week. The problem was definitely me! My kids could play LEGOs™ endlessly or create fantastic cities of recyclable materials. But, I couldn't handle not having something to report at the end of the day, something to record in our Daily Log. I know it was the auditory-sequential part of me yearning to show accomplishment and advancement, but unschooling was sheer torture for me. I do, however, highly recommend a period of unschooling for children who have recently left damaging school environments to pursue homeschooling. I've seen numerous situations where the children needed time to, literally, detox. They need to get all that happened in a bad situation behind them before they are able to move on to the next phase of their academic careers. (For more information on unschooling, I recommend the books by John Holt found at www.holtgws.com.)

Afterschooling

Afterschooling is just that, additional time spent after-school learning. This is a great opportunity to help your children master what is being taught in the classroom by incorporating visual techniques with material that has already been presented to them auditorally. Some examples would include creating timelines and other visuals to help remember dates, names and places of the historical information they are studying; memorizing math facts in visual and humorous ways; and helping with spelling words by creating them on cards in color and with humorous stories to memorize—as a picture—how the word is spelled. Afterschooling, like homeschooling, has the distinct advantage of being created with your children's specific needs in mind.

The downfall of afterschooling is time. Following a seven- or eight-hour day in classes, the topsy-turvy kid will often be hard-pressed to endure any more studying. With today's kids enrolled in sports, music, scouting and other afterschool activities, families may struggle to find time to incorporate afterschooling into their lives.

In Singapore, nearly all children work with a tutor after school. Tutoring is another form of afterschooling that should be considered when a child is struggling in school or needs added depth and enrichment in a particular subject.

Now that you know some options, stay open-minded about choosing among them. No decision is permanent and, unless you move to some utterly remote village in another country, you can always return to traditional schooling. For us, the boys' educational option has been a year-by-year—sometimes semester-by-semester—decision.

Maybe If We Ignore It, They'll Outgrow It?

I once received an e-mail from a website visitor asking me if a support group existed for parents of children with this "disorder" and advice on how to "cure" her child. Once I got my blood pressure back under control, I responded that a preferred learning style should not be thought of as a disorder any more than preferred handedness would be considered a physical handicap. I wrote that there certainly was no "cure" available for this child other than that the adults in her life would need to accept and honor her for the gifts she had and the manner in which her brain performed best. I hope I sounded more positive and less angered in my response than I do here, but I am deeply concerned for the topsy-turvy children of the world whose parents and teachers are trying to cure them. The strength of their right hemi-spheres is something these children were born with and has the potential to be a tremendous asset to them and to the world! It is a gift they will possess all their lives so I propose we all embrace it, honor it and teach these children in the manner in which they learn best.

> After reading more about this learning style I realized that the methods I used behind people's backs were not something to be ashamed of but to be proud that I knew how to help myself learn.

Successful visual-spatial adults throughout history include composers, artists, scientists, inventors, actors and more (see Tom West's **In the Mind's Eye** for some examples). All, at some point, were honored for their visual-spatial gifts. Some did not have recognition until late in life, even posthumously. By honoring our visual-spatial children now, we plant seeds for success in their academic careers and beyond.

What about the future of traditional schooling?

The great artists and musicians, scientists and inventors, actors and playwrights throughout modern history are testament to the strengths of the right hemisphere. Their individual stories of perseverance give hope to visual-spatial learners everywhere. It is important to note that the biographies of a great many of these successful men and women often feature non-traditional schooling and/or "late blooming" that allowed these eminent contributors to excel. Few visual-spatial learners throughout history have been able to emerge from traditional academic experiences, most turned to home-schooling or other alternative learning environments that allowed them to tap into their truly amazing gifts. Success for visual-spatial learners in auditory-sequential classrooms remains a rare event.

How is it possible that we can honor the gifts that artists, musicians and inventors bring us, but not create an academic environment in which they can blossom and succeed? Why must such gifts be forced to endure, to persevere against a system that does not understand or honor them? Their pain can be intense.

It is time to help create classrooms and learning environments that listen and respond to the needs of all students, auditory-sequential and visual-spatial. To do so takes nothing away from the learning environment for auditory-sequential learners, it only enhances it. Adding visual presentations and hands-on experiences of new information reinforces the learning—and the fun—for everyone.

First, we must share an understanding that not all students learn the same. Each of us is equipped with a left and right hemisphere. Some of us use more of one hemisphere than the other. Some, exaggeratedly so. Did I mention that research has shown that *at least* one-third of the population is strongly visual-spatial, roughly a fourth is strongly auditory-sequential and the remainder of the population relies on both hemispheres equally to learn and understand information? (OK, only about fifteen times by now, but it's really an important statistic!) Of that final group who rely on both of their hemispheres equally, 30% show a preference toward visual-spatial learning while only 15% show a preference for auditory-sequential learning. This means that there are far too many visual-spatial learners in any given classroom, at any given age, to be ignored. Topsy-turvy kids unite! Your time has come! You are slowly becoming a force that cannot be overlooked.

Without even having to identify each student's learning style, a teacher can accurately assume that at least one-third of the class is visual-spatial. That's at least ten students in a class of thirty. Once your children's teachers understand that the methods used to successfully reach them, as visual-spatial learners, are also effective for reaching auditory-sequential learners, it should not be a big leap to create accommodations for topsy-turvy students. What are the accommodations? They are as simple as adding visuals to every new bit of information students are given. Some teachers are doing a wonderful job teaching VSLs. Listen to this:

> His homeroom teacher discovered that he was a very talented writer, as well. I truly believe it was her method of teaching that brought out this latent ability in O. She seemed to be a very visual person herself, and used lots of color-coding and visual diagrams in her instruction. Looking beyond the bad handwriting and total lack of organization skills, she could see

the amazing insight this little boy possessed, and affection-
ately referred to him as "the absent-minded professor." Best
of all, she truly appreciated his quirky, if not outright twisted,
sense of humor.

Visual-spatial learners remember what they see so the
use of color and size is very important. Whether it's spelling
words that use different colors and exaggerated height to call
attention to the challenging part of the word (See Chapter 5
for examples) or math facts that use numbers disguised as
various characters drawn large and colorfully, visual-spatial
learners are more likely to retain that image—and recall it
later—than if just straight text and regular numbers are
presented. These are techniques you can easily use at home
and can ask your children's teachers to readily incorporate
into their classrooms, as well.

Career choices

When we asked G at 3 what he wanted to be when he grew up,
he said "A Shapes Lovist," someone who loves shapes for a
living.

Topsy-turvy children will have a wide range of available
career choices awaiting them, many of which have not even
been created yet. The widespread deployment of computers in
every aspect of our lives will be of continued benefit to the
next generation of visual-spatial adults who seem to come
into the world pre-wired with the knowledge of how best to
manipulate such equipment.

Encourage your children to explore future careers that
utilize their skills set to the greatest advantage. This would
include pursuing art, music or drama as not only a passion
but as a means of earning a living. Or following their heart's
desires in higher level mathematics, science, invention and
architecture, surgery, aeronautics, cartography, areas that
make use of the visual-spatial learner's ability to think in
multiple dimensions and from varied perspectives. Any
restrictions to what they want to pursue, as adults, are
simply the limitations they place on their own imagination.

That's all for now

I hope that if you have learned anything in this book, it
has been to honor your children for the gifts these visual-
spatial learners possess and to help them succeed academically
by providing an environment in which they can thrive. As more
topsy-turvy kids are identified and more classrooms are modified to incorporate strategies that will successfully reach these
visual-spatial learners, their differences will become less
problematic, their gifts more revered.

I once joked with Linda that perhaps bookstores of the
future would feature self-help books for a generation that had
forgotten how to think and learn sequentially. Sort of a "World
Taken Over by Visual-Spatial Learners" scenario. My joke
became a cartoon featured in Chapter 5 of **Upside-Down
Brilliance**:

I hope I've done what I set out to do here: help parents in
navigating the course before them and the challenges in
raising topsy-turvy kids. If you have suggestions you'd like to
share, tips that have worked with your children or more
questions than I've answered, I'd love to hear from you. You'll
find me as "Alex" on the Web at www.gifteddevelopment.com

or www.visualspatial.org. Also, at the Visual-Spatial Resource website, you'll find continuing updates of relevant articles, upcoming conferences, information on bringing speakers in to your school, and more.

Thank you and best of luck to you and your children!

References

☞ **FYI - All URLs (web addresses) that are enclosed in quotes, are to be considered continuous and do not contain spaces.**

Gordon, S. (2003, November 25). Right's wrong for speech development. *Healthfinder-your guide to reliable health.* Retrieved January 6, 2004, from "http://www.healthfinder.gov/news/newsstory.asp?docID=516194"

Gifted Development Center
www.gifteddevelopment.com

Haas, S. C. (2003) Classroom Identification of Visual-Spatial Learners. Gifted Education Communicator, 19.

The works of unschooler promoter John Holt
www.holtgws.com

Maxwell, E. (2003) Wholes and Patterns: Reading Help for Struggling Visual-Spatial Learners. *Gifted Education Communicator,* 22-23.

National Home Educators Network
http://nhen.org

Pearson, J. (1995). *Drawing on the Inventive Mind: Exercises in Thinking, Language and Self-Esteem.* Los Angeles, CA: Creative Thinking Programs.

Pearson, J. (1999). *Drawing Out the Best in Your Students.* Los Angeles, CA: Creative Thinking Programs.

Silverman, L.K. (2002) *Upside-Down Brilliance: The Visual-Spatial Learner.* Denver, CO: DeLeon Publishing.

Visual-Spatial Resource
www.visualspatial.org

Walker, A. (1998) *Memorize in minutes: The times tables.* Prosser, WA: Krimsten Publishing.

West, T. G. (1997). *In the mind's eye: Visual thinkers, gifted people with dyslexia and other learning difficulties, computer images, and the ironies of creativity.* (Updated ed.). Amherst, NY: Prometheus.

Appendix A
Resources for Visual-Spatial Learners

ABC's of the Writing Process, Specific Graphic Organizer Links "www.angelfire.com/wi/writingprocess/specificgos.html"	Complex graphic organizers, including diagrams, webs, etc.
Concept Mapping "www.uwp.edu.academic/stec/MBASC/Concept_Mapping/concept.mapping.faq.html"	Instructions on how to present material in a more visual manner
Creative Publications/Wright Group www.wrightgroup.com 1-800-523-2371	Attribute Blocks, Balances, Base Ten Blocks, Marilyn Burns' Math Books, Fraction manipulatives, Geoboards, Hundreds Boards, Pattern Blocks, Tangrams (Lots of great stuff plus work/idea books)
Critical & Creative Thinking for the Gifted www.criticalthinking.com 1-800-458-4849	Critical thinking books and software across all subject areas and grade levels
Cuisenaire-Dale Seymour www.etacuisenaire.com 1-800-445-5985	Cuisenaire Rods™; Excellent math manipulatives and creative visual-spatial materials that extend through Grade 12
Delta Education www.delta-education.com 1-800-258-1302	Math and science products
fLearn www.fLearn.com 303-499-4386 1-800-499-4386	Advice regarding software for math, science, language arts, social studies, etc.; Wipe-off Hundreds Boards; Fractiles™; Zometool®; Triangular Flash Cards (multiplication & division); great science equipment
Graphic Organizers www.graphic.org/goindex.html	Venn diagrams, webs, and more
Hands-On Equations www.borenson.com 1-800-993-6284	A visual and kinesthetic teaching system for introducing algebraic concepts to students in grades 3 to 8
Inspiration Software www.inspiration.com 1-800-877-4292	Inspiration (software for mind maps, Grades 5-12); Kidspiration for younger children (Grades K-4)

Math-U-See www.mathusee.com 1-888-854-MATH 1-800-225-6654 in Canada	K-12 math program that uses visual-spatial methods to teach mathematics; instructional videos; manipulative; student and teacher textbooks
Mindware www.mindwareonline.com 1-800-999-0398	Collection of spatial games: mazes, puzzles, Tower of Hanoi™, Rubik's™ Cubes, Fractiles™, building equipment, math, science and geography materials
Multiplication www.multiplication.com	Multiplication made easy through the use of silly stories and cartoons
Prufrock Press www.prufrock.com 1-800-240-0333	Mind Benders® (Anita Harnadek) Math Mind Benders®, Grades 3-12 Science experiment books, Grades 2-9
Science, Math & Gifted SMG Products Catalog www.smgproducts.com (715) 235-1840	Science toys and resource books, critical thinking; math activities; gifted resources; puzzles; strategy games; Continuo™; Rhombo Continuo™; mysteries; lateral thinking; logic; problem solving
Teach with Movies www.teachwithmovies.org	Resource for using movies to teach in a variety of subject areas
Teacher Ideas Press www.lu.com/tips/ 1-800-225-5800	Creating Success in the Classroom: Visual Organizers And How to Use Them (Tarquin & Walker, 1996)
Teaching Company www.teachco.com	College courses on videotape and audiotape for advanced learners
Zephyr Press www.zephyrpress.com 1-800-232-2187	Mapping Inner Space (webs) Smart-Rope Jingles; Rappin' and Rhymin'
Zometool, Inc. www.zometool.com 303-733-2880 1-800-966-3386	Lesson plans for using the Zome System® in the classroom

Recommended Books for Visual-Spatial Learners

Burchers, S., Burchers, M., & Burchers, B. (1998). *Vocabulary cartoons: Building an educated vocabulary with visual mnemonics.* Punta Gorda, FL: New Monic Books. [314-C Tamiani Trail, Punta Gorda, FL 33950 (941) 575-6669]

Buzan, T. (1983). *Use Both Sides of Your Brain* (revised). New York: E. P. Dutton.

Clark, F., & Clark, C. (with M. Vogel). (1989). *Hassle-Free Homework: A Six-Week Plan for Parents and Children to Take the Pain out of Homework.* New York: Doubleday.

Dixon, J. P. (1983). *The Spatial Child.* Springfield, IL: Charles C. Thomas.

Freed, J., & Parsons, L. (1998). *Right-Brained Children in a Left-Brained World: Unlocking the Potential of your ADD Child.* New York: Simon & Schuster.

Levitt, P. M., Burger, D. A., & Guralnick, E. S. (1985). *The Weighty Word Book.* Longmont, CO: Bookmaker's Guild.

Parks, S., & Black, H. (1998). *Building Thinking Skills: Book 2* (2nd ed.). Pacific Grove, CA: Critical Thinking Books and Software.

Parks, S., & Black, H. (2000). *Building Thinking Skills: Beginning Figural.* Pacific Grove, CA: Critical Thinking Books and Software.

Pearson, J. (1995). *Drawing on the Inventive Mind: Exercises in Thinking, Language and Self-Esteem.* Los Angeles, CA: Creative Thinking Programs.

Pearson, J. (1999). *Drawing Out the Best in Your Students.* Los Angeles, CA: Creative Thinking Programs.

Silverman, L.K. (2002). *Upside-Down Brilliance: The Visual-Spatial Learner.* Denver, CO: DeLeon Publishing.

Vitale, B. (1982). *Unicorns Are Real.* Rolling Hills Estates, CA: Jalmar Press.

Williams, L. V. (1983). *Teaching for the Two-Sided Mind.* Englewood Cliffs, NJ: Prentice-Hall.

West, T. G. (1997). *In the mind's eye: Visual thinkers, gifted people with dyslexia and other learning difficulties, computer images, and the ironies of creativity.* (Updated ed.). Amherst, NY: Prometheus.

Appendix B

Homeschooling Resources

Creative Homeschooling for the Gifted: A Resource Guide, by Lisa Rivero

Homeschooling for Excellence, by David and Micki Colfax

The Well-Trained Mind, by Jessie Wise and Susan Wise Bauer

Homeschool Your Child For Free, by Gold & Zielinski

What Your Xth Grader Should Know, by E.D. Hirsch

Home Learning Year by Year, by Rebecca Rupp

The Complete Home Learning Source, by Rebecca Rupp

Family Matters: Why Homeschooling Makes Sense, by David Guterson

The Successful Homeschool Family Handbook: A Creative and Stress-Free Approach to Homeschooling, by Dorothy and Raymond Moore

The Homeschoolers' Handbook: From Preschool to High School: A Parent's Guide, by Mary Griffith

And What About College?, By Cafi Cohen

Real Lives: Eleven Teenageers Who Don't Go To School, by Grace Llewellyn

Best Websites for Homeschoolers

A to Z Home's Cool Homeschooling Web Site
www.gomilpitas.com/homeschooling

Classroom Direct
www.classroomdirect.com

Half.com (now parented by eBay)
www.half.com

Homeschool Central
www.homeschoolcentral.com

Home School Legal Defense Association
www.hslda.org

Internet Resources for Homeschooling Gifted Students
"www.gifteddevelopment.com/Articles/
Homeschool_Int_Res.htm"

Middle School Net
www.middleschool.net
Middle School Curriculum for virtually any subject

National Home Educator's Network
www.nhen.org
Rules and laws for every state, links to getting started and more

National Standards for Public Education
www.mcrel.org

Rainbow Resource Center
www.rainbowresource.com

Scholastic
www.scholastic.com

Smart Kit at Home
www.smartkidathome.com

State Standards
www.statestandards.com

TAGMAX
www.tagfam.org

The Upside-Down School Room
www.upsidedownschoolroom.com

Zenger Media
www.socialstudies.com

Distance Learning Information

American High School
www.iit.edu/~american
High School correspondence courses

Athena University
www.athena.edu
K-12 Academy, on-line courses

Barnes & Noble
www.barnesandnobleuniversity.com
50+ courses from poetry to finance, free!

Brigham Young University Independent Study

> www.coned.byu.edu/is/index2.htm
>
> Correspondence and on-line courses for high school students

California Virtual University

> www.california.edu
>
> 2,000+ on-line courses

Calvert Home School Instruction Dept.

> www.calvertschool.org
>
> Complete curricula for grads K-8 410-243-5030

Cambridge Academy

> www.homeschool.com/Mall/Cambridge/CambridgeAcad.html

Capella University

> www.capellauniversity.edu
>
> 400+ online, undergraduate and graduate courses

Child U

> www.childu.com
>
> Complete online curriculum for grades 1-8

Christa McAuliffe Academy

> www.cmacademy.org
>
> Online with off-line study, grades K-12

Chrysalis School

> www.chrysalis-school.com
>
> Individual courses or full-program, grades K-12

Citizen's High School

> www.citizenschool.com
>
> Correspondence using standard high school texts

Clonlara Home Based Education Program

> www.clonlara.org
>
> Grades K-12, on-line thru Clonlara Compuhigh

Colorado Virtual Charter School

> www.covcs.org
>
> Using curriculum from K12, currently serving grades K-5

Compu High (part of Clonlara)

> www.compuhigh.com
>
> On-line accredited high school courses

Dennison Academy On-Line Internet School
>   www.denisononline.com
>   Individual courses or full program, grades 7+

Distance Learning on the Net
>   www.hoyle.com/distance.htm
>   Lists of available courses by Glenn Hoyle

Distance Learning Research Network
>   "www.wested.org/tie/dlrn/k12de.html"
>   Links to various kinds of distance learning institutions

ECollege
>   www.ecolloege.com
>   Search engine that links to numerous colleges for specific
>   degrees, on-line courses

Eldorado Academy
>   www.eldoradoacademy.org
>   Private, distance learning school, K-12

Electronic High School
>   www.ehs.uen.org
>   On-line high school classes

Florida High School
>   www.fhs.net

Foundation for On-Line Learning
>   "www.infinet.com/~ndonald/links/fol.html"
>   Free home-educator taught courses

Greenwood Institute
>   www.greenwoodinstitute.org
>   Homeschool support programs for disabled kids, especially
>   those with dyslexia

High School Hub
>   www.highschoolhub.org
>   Free, on-line high school level courses, variety of subjects

Homeschoolers of Maine
>   "www.homeschool-
>   maine.org/high_school_&_beyond.htm#FreeOnlineCourses"
>   Free on-line courses

Home Study International
>   www.his.edu

Pre-K –12 Christian correspondence courses sponsored by Seventh Day Adventist Church

ICS High School Program

www.icslearn.com/ICS
Complete high school distance learning program

Ignite the Fire Homeschooling Website

"www.ignitethefire.com/placement.html"
Free AP courses and curriculum materials under "Free Firewood" section

Independence High School

www.independentlearning.com
Kids design their own curricula.

Indiana University School of Continuing Studies

www.scs.indiana.edu
Complete high school program.

Interactive Learning Network

www.iln.net
High School and college-level courses

Internet Academy

www.iacademy.org
Complete K-12 curriculum

Internet Home School

www.internethomeschool.com
On-Line programs, grades K-12

Internet University

www.internet-university.com
Instructor-led, web-based courses, college-level

K-12

www.k12-com

Keystone National High School

www.keystonehighschool.com
Correspondence, or "eSchool" on-line programs

Kolbe Academy Home School

www.kolbe.org
Classical Catholic curriculum by correspondence, grades K-12

Laurel Springs School
>   www.laurelsprings.com
>   Project-based or textbook-based and on-line courses, K-12

Louisiana State University Independent Study
>   www.is.lsu.edu/highschool
>   High-school level correspondence courses

Moore Foundation Academy
>   www.moorefoundation.com
>   Christian project-focused programs, K-12

North Atlantic Regional High School
>   www.narsonline.com
>   Receive high school diploma from Maine for homeschool classes

NewPromise.com
>   www.mindedge.com
>   Database of on-line college courses, searchable by subject or
>   institution

North Dakota Division of Independent Study
>   www.dis.dpi.state.nd.us
>   Print-based or on-line courses, grades 5-12

Northwestern University Center for Talent Development
>   www.ctd.northwestern.edu
>   High school honors classes

The Online College Classroom
>   www.leahi.kcc.hawaii.edu
>   Directory of colleges offering distance learning and online
>   classes, sponsored by Hawaiian college

PA Homeschoolers Advanced Placement Courses
>   www.pahomeschoolers.com/courses
>   On-line AP classes

Seton Home Study School
>   www.setonhome.org
>   Classical Catholic curriculum, grades K-12

Stanford Education Program for Gifted Youth
>   www.epgy.stanford.edu
>   Computer-based distance learning including math, science,
>   English, computer science, Grades elementary through high
>   school

Study Web
> www.studyweb.com/Teaching_Resources
> List of correspondence schools

Texas Tech University
> www.dec.ttu.edu
> Comprehensive curriculum of on-line and correspondence courses, grades K-12

Tutornet
> www.tutornet.com
> On-line virtual classrooms, elementary thru college

University of Arizona
> www.eu.arizona.edu/correso
> Independent study through correspondence: elementary, middle and high school programs

University of Missouri Independent Study
> www.cdis.missouri.edu
> Comprehensive high school curriculum through correspondence or online courses

University of Nebraska Independent Study High School
> www.dcs.unl.edu/disted
> Complete high school curriculum, correspondence or online.

University of Oklahoma Independent Study
> www.occe.ou.edu
> 70+ high school correspondence courses

University of Washington
> www.extension.washington.edu/dl
> On-line classes available , but cant' earn degree

University of Wisconsin Learning Innovations Center
> www.learn.wisconsin.edu
> High school courses by correspondence

Virtual School for the Gifted
> www.vsg.edu.au
> Based in Australia, features variety of 9-week classes, grades 4-12

Westbridge Academy
"www.flash.net/~wx3o/westbridge/index.htm"
College prepatory school for academically advanced homeschoolers

Willoway Cyber School
www.willoway.com
Grades 7-12

Appendix C

<u>Survival Checklist for Parents</u>

_____ Meet with teachers early in the school year to discuss known preferred learning styles

_____ Offer to help create hands-on learning materials for use in the classroom

_____ Offer to work with children in older grades to use humor, color, emphasis to remember math facts, historical data, etc.

_____ Read _Upside-Down Brilliance: The Visual-Spatial Learner_ – offer it to your children's teachers

_____ Remember to think big picture first, smaller details last

_____ Help VSL students create visual images that stick!

_____ Make everything silly, big, colorful and fun!

_____ Have your child ask if lecture outlines/overviews are available prior to class

_____ Can lectures be tape recorded?

_____ Teach whole word reading, not phonics

_____ Teach your child to speed read

_____ Help teach note taking in pictures

_____ Create tricks for memorizing spelling words

_____ Teach your children keyboarding

_____ Find visual tricks to help math facts stick

_____ Keep it challenging – don't let the right hemisphere check out

_____ Double check that the picture of what you want done matches your child's image of the request – never assume!

_____ Experiment with ways to keep your children focused: manipulative objects, PVC pipes, hats, etc.

_____ Visit office supply stores for organizational products

_____ Make sure you have their attention

_____ Maintain regular homework, TV, computer and chore schedules

_____ Listen if your children ask about other schooling options – consider all avenues

Index

"Upside-Down" learners, viii

V

Vision
  issues, 31–32, 67
  therapy, 32
Visualization, 2–6, 8–10, 15, 23, 37, 47. *See also* Material memorable, making; Pictures
Visual-Spatial Identifier, 10
Visual-Spatial Resource website, 102

W

West, Tom, 98
Whole-part learning, 7, 15-16, 58–60, 66, 77–78, 79–82, 89
Whole-word reading, 7, 60, 70–73
Words, rhyming, 56, 71, 81
Work, showing, 2, 6, 82, 89
Writing, 75–78

Y

Yeats, William Butler, 93

Z

Z-like patterns, 72

Knowledge is power....

DeLeon Publishing, Inc.

Empowering the world one book at a time.

P.O. Box 461027, Denver, CO 80246   www.deleonpub.com

❦ ❦ ❦

Full-Sized Forms Available for download online!

To download full-sized 8.5 x 11 inch reproducible forms used in this book, please visit http://www.deleonpub.com/authors.html or http://www.visualspatial.org.

The forms are in PDF format. You will need to have Adobe[®] Acrobat Reader installed on your computer in order to view them. Please visit Adobe's website at www.adobe.com to download their free PDF reader program.

❦ ❦ ❦

Other books offered from DeLeon Publishing:

Title:	Format:	Author:	ISBN:	Price:
Upside-Down Brilliance	SC	L.K.Silverman	1-932186-00-X	24.95
Raising Topsy-Turvy Kids	SC	A.S.Golon	1-932186-08-5	14.95
Empowering Gifted Minds	SC	B.J.Gilman	1-932186-02-6	26.95
My Life Experiences With Children	SC	A.Roeper	1-932186-06-9	17.95
Across Time And Space	VHS	Searchlight Films	NA	29.95
Druidawn	SC	M.Darnell	1-4010-4472-7	19.95
Legends of Druidawn	SC	M.Darnell	NA	69.90
LOD Game Only	BNDR	M.Darnell	NA	49.95
A Time To Fly Free	SC	S.Tolan	0-689-71420-3	3.95
A Case Of Brilliance	SC	R.Hein	1-55395-224-3	16.99

Please visit our website for more information on any title.

Ask for them at your local bookstore or online at www.deleonpub.com.